REBELS ON THE RIO GRANDE

Peticolas's self-portrait drawn while resting in quarters following the New Mexico campaign, July 1862. (Arizona Historical Society)

Rebels on the Rio Grande

The Civil War Journal
❧ of A. B. Peticolas ❧

Edited by
Don E. Alberts

University of New Mexico Press
Albuquerque

Library of Congress Cataloging in Publication Data

Peticolas, A. B. (Alfred Brown), 1838–1915.
  Rebels on the Rio Grande.

  Bibliography: p.
  Includes index.
  1. Peticolas, A. B. (Alfred Brown), 1838–1915. 2. United States—History—Civil War, 1861–1865—Personal narratives—Confederate. 3. New Mexico—History—Civil War, 1861–1865—Personal narratives, Confederate. 4. Confederate States of America. Army—Biography. 5. Soldiers—Texas—Biography. I. Alberts, Don E. II. Title.
E605.P47 1984   973.7'31 [B]   84-17237
ISBN 0-8263-0766-3
ISBN 0-8263-0773-6 (pbk.)

International Standard Book Number 0-8263-0766-3 (cloth).
International Standard Book Number 0-8263-0773-6 (paper).
Library of Congress Catalog Card Number 84-17237.
First edition

Contents

To my wife,
Rosemary Chilton Jones,
companion on the trail of the Texans

Preface

The journal presented herein is a remarkable document, especially when the circumstances under which it was written are considered. Alfred B. Peticolas often made entries by the light of a candle or campfire, at the end of a day of marching through extremely rough country; with little food, and that cooked by the soldiers themselves; and during a season in New Mexico that often brings very cold temperatures along with snow and sandstorms.

Even under such conditions, Peticolas wrote well, and as a result, little actual editing has been required. In some cases the spelling of place names in New Mexico has been corrected if such correction makes the journal more understandable. Likewise, some punctuation has been added in the interest of readability, but such changes have been minimized in order to preserve the original "flavor."

This is actually the second volume of Peticolas's Civil War journal. The first volume, which described his experiences in Texas as the Sibley Brigade was being recruited and trained, and the journey of the brigade across West Texas and into New Mexico leading up to the day of the Battle of Valverde, was lost. It was with Peticolas's belongings when the Texan wagon train was blown up and burned by Union forces during the Battle of Glorieta. He was greatly distressed after visiting the site of the burned train and determining that, indeed, his work was destroyed. However, one of his companions had made an abbreviated copy of his first volume during the journey to New Mexico, and Peticolas made a copy of that copy later when he had the time. Somehow, the copied first volume did not survive with the second and third volumes. In spite of persistent rumors of its existence, my extensive search for that volume proved fruitless, as did a similar effort by Dr. Darlis Miller, of New Mexico State University.

Peticolas's second volume covers the entire active campaign in New Mexico, however, and offers an unparalleled view of soldier life during that little-known episode of the Civil War. His third volume deals with subsequent service in the Texas and Louisiana campaigns later in the war. By that time, battles and military life had become much less exciting and interesting to the young soldier, and consequently, his last volume contributes less to our knowledge of his times than does this second volume.

That so much of the wartime Peticolas journal and its accompanying sketches survived is indeed fortunate, since they are without a doubt the best personal records kept by any participant in the Confederate invasion of New Mexico.

In completing this extensive project, I realize how dependent I was on the help, expertise, and encouragement of other interested people.

El Paso historian Marion Grinstead contributed her considerable knowledge of the Fort Craig area and helped make initial contacts leading to publication of the Peticolas journal. New Mexico's outstanding historian, Dr. Marc Simmons, also helped significantly with advice and encouragement, as did Linda Frye, the gracious and enthusiastic owner of Pigeon's Ranch, at Glorieta. In Las Cruces, Dr. Darlis Miller generously shared her knowledge of the Peticolas material and its missing volume.

In Victoria, Texas, Dr. Robert Shook copied and shared manuscript holdings in his local history collection of the Victoria College. Other Texans, descendants of A. B. Peticolas, were also indispensable. Marian H. Martin, his great-granddaughter, of Azle, Texas, contributed valuable genealogical information. I am much obligated to her and to El Paso attorney William C. Peticolas, grandson of the Confederate soldier and owner of the Peticolas Civil War journal. Mr. Peticolas generously granted permission to publish the journal and loaned the original volumes to me so that accurate transcriptions could be made. Without his support and friendship, this project would have been impossible.

As usual, Dr. Sara Jackson, of the National Historical Publications Commission, was a major helper. Sara found many vital primary sources in the holdings of the National Archives and contributed them, as well as constant encouragement, to this work.

In the Albuquerque area, several people gave important assistance. Byron Johnson, curator of history at the Albuquerque Museum, helped with information on the local Civil War military post and with relevant photos and sources. Dee Brecheisen, New Mexico's foremost relic hunter, and an excellent historian in his own right, generously showed me significant Civil War sites and camps used by A. B. Peticolas and the Sibley Brigade. Dee also loaned valuable publications from his extensive collection. Another enthusiastic relic hunter and researcher, Dr. Philip Mead, was absolutely indispensable. As companion around campfires in the "barren, inhospitable wastes of New Mexico" and along many miles tracing the Texans' route in four-wheel-drive vehicles and afoot, Phil Mead's enthusiasm never faltered, even when mine did. He shared with me the job of making the original journal transcription and in interpreting in its light the information we gained on numerous field expeditions. Finally, he applied his editing expertise to the manuscript, proofreading it and making many valuable improvements in style and content. His efforts are greatly appreciated.

My wife, Rosemary, and my children, Jackie and Clint, were my major supporters. They endured periods of inevitable neglect and shared periods of exciting activity as we followed Peticolas's journey through New Mexico and Texas. Their enthusiasm and encouragement were vital ingredients in the completion of this work. To them, and to all the others who helped, thanks.

Don Alberts
Albuquerque, 1983

Introduction

To a United States unfamiliar with large-scale warfare, the year 1861 brought the prospect of adventure, along with extraordinary military campaigns, to amateur soldiers North and South. Little of the grimness realized later in the Civil War was apparent as young men eagerly enlisted for active service.

One of these eager volunteers was Alfred Brown Peticolas, a young lawyer from Victoria, Texas, who joined other troops from his state for one of the more unusual campaigns conducted during the Civil War—the Confederate invasion of New Mexico. In many ways typical of other frontier soldiers with whom he had enlisted (he could ride, shoot, and endure considerable hardship), Peticolas was in even more ways different, perhaps even unique. He was well educated, a natural leader, and an inveterate observer of his companions and surroundings as well as his own feelings. In addition, he was an excellent diarist and artist, recording his impressions of the 1861–62 New Mexico campaign in word and sketch.

A. B. Peticolas was not a native of the Texas frontier. The fifth of seven children, he was born in Richmond, Virginia, on 27 May 1838, to Mildred Warner Brown and Julius Adolphus Peticolas. Apparently, the family was reasonably affluent; certainly, nowhere in A. B. Peticolas's journals is there mention of deprivation of any kind during his early years. His father died when Alfred was eight years old, leaving his mother, and later an uncle, Robert Brown, responsible for his education and care.[1] They neglected neither, and the

---

1. Pedigree Chart and Peticolas Family Genealogy, Merrow E. Sorley, comp. This information was furnished by Marian H. Martin, of Azle, Texas. Mrs. Martin is a great-granddaughter of A. B. Peticolas. Copy in editor's collection.

boy received excellent schooling after the family moved to nearby Petersburg. Peticolas later remembered his youth in Petersburg with great pleasure, especially Sunday attendance at the Tab Street Church with his mother.[2]

Uncle Robert was an attorney practicing in Amherst County, west of Petersburg.[3] His example very likely convinced young Peticolas that he, too, wanted to become a lawyer. By his late teens, A. B. Peticolas had determined that he would study law, and that determination became the motivating force in his life for several years thereafter. After finishing his public-school education in Petersburg in the late 1850s, Alfred moved with his mother to Amherst County, in the vicinity of Lynchburg. Whether or not he and Mrs. Peticolas moved in with her brother Robert is not clear from surviving journals, but A. B. Peticolas soon decided on an independent course of action.[4]

Public education had not extended to rural Amherst County. Schooling was available to students whose parents could afford it, however, but it was provided by private teachers and tutors. To support himself and to make possible his study of law, Peticolas opened his own small school to serve part of the fairly heavily populated countryside near Lynchburg. There he rented a building for the school, as well as living and office space for himself. The number of "scholars" attending his school varied, but by the 1858–59 session, he had approximately two dozen subscribers for his services, and in addition, he tutored older students who could not or would not attend regular classes.[5]

With no compulsory attendance laws, the young schoolmaster was often frustrated by absentees, but quickly learned the techniques of enforcing his own rules regarding not only attendance, but study habits and lesson presentations. He was also perturbed occasionally when parents were tardy in making tuition payments to him or wanted to withdraw their children from school without good reason. As a result, by the end of the school year in July 1859,

---

2. Ibid.

3. Alfred B. Peticolas, "Journal of A. B. Peticolas, May–July 1859," MSS, Local History Collection, Victoria College, Victoria, Texas, entry for 2 May 1859. Copy in editor's collection.

4. Ibid., entries for 2, 4 May 1859.

5. Ibid., entries for 12, 19 May 1859.

A. B. Peticolas's self-portrait, drawn while he was a twenty-year-old schoolmaster in Amherst County, Virginia. (Arizona Historical Society)

3

he was "very weary of the task of teaching such dull, lazy scholars ... with a few exceptions."[6]

From his own hand we have valuable insights into Peticolas's character, as well as the times in which he lived. He described himself as "an inveterate scribbler," and by the time he was teaching near Lynchburg at age twenty, he had formed the habit of keeping a detailed journal of "the little minutiae of my life."[7] He also enjoyed sketching scenes and objects around, and although not a trained artist, he was quite skilled in his pastime. He continued writing and sketching at least through the Civil War years, and possibly longer. Only one prewar journal and a few sketches are known to have survived from his life as a young man in Virginia. Of three wartime journal volumes, two have been located, along with a collection of sketches made during and after the New Mexico campaign. In addition, Peticolas sketched many scenes around prewar and postwar Victoria, Texas, and several of those drawings survive.

From these journals and drawings, we see the young schoolmaster as a tall (6'4"), thoughtful person of varied talents. During his first year as a teacher, Peticolas wrote a novel and submitted it to the *Southern Literary Messenger* in Richmond. Unfortunately, he never commented on its theme or ultimate publication fate. He played the accordion and traded for his own instrument while in Amherst County.[8] He was also familiar with firearms, hunting squirrels in the nearby woods with some success. Although he owned no horses, he had the use of several belonging to his landlord. There is no evidence that Peticolas was deeply interested in horses, but he became an adequate, if not enthusiastic, rider.[9] Peticolas considered himself a religious man and gave some thought to the matter. In his everyday life, however, religion played a very small part. He could be classed as a freethinker. For him, regular church attendance was mainly a social and intellectual treat, giving him the opportunity to analyze the preacher's sermon as well as to visit with friends.[10]

Strangely, for a young man so interested in the law, Peticolas had relatively little interest in contemporary politics. The great

---

6. Ibid., entries for 7, 22 July 1859.

7. Ibid., entry for 2 May 1859.

8. Ibid., entries for 2, 14, May and 17 June 1859.

9. Ibid., entries for 7, 13 May and 16 July 1859.

10. Ibid., entries for 8, 22 May and 12 June 1859.

Scenes of Amherst County, Virginia, by A. B. Peticolas during 1854 and 1856. (Marian H. Martin Collection)

issues of the day—sectionalism, slavery, states' rights, and abolition —are not even mentioned in his 1859 journal. To some extent that might have been because he was too young to vote; he turned twenty-one the day after Virginia's gubernatorial primary election in May 1859. In addition, his moderate political inclinations may have contributed to his disinterest in the major issues. Peticolas preferred that the Whig candidate win against the Democrats' incumbent governor John Letcher, but he was realistic enough to realize that "this state is so thoroughly democratic [*sic*] that I think Letcher will certainly be elected. . . ." His dislike for Democrats was again apparent during June, when that party's celebrated campaigner, William "Extra Billy" Smith, appeared at an extensive barbecue in Lynchburg. Peticolas was invited, but declined since he had "no desire to partake with the great unwashed."[11] Even later, as civil war approached and became a reality, there is no evidence that lawyer Peticolas was active in local Texas politics or was much concerned with the immediate questions of secession or possible treason that affected him directly.

But if Peticolas thought little about Virginia politics, he was deeply committed to his law studies and had given considerable thought to his reasons for wanting to become a lawyer and to his prospects for success. He had great self-confidence and felt that it would be "strange if in the course of half a dozen years I do not become a first-rate lawyer. I believe I have the capability, and with a little practice I expect I shall be able to speak very well."[12] He was a realist, however, and also observed, "Time will show whether I have that principle [success] about me, and while I hope that I have, I am not confident that I shall, for close observers of human nature have said that *circumstances make men*."[13]

Before the Civil War, becoming a lawyer could be a relatively informal procedure. Typically, it included reading and studying certain more-or-less classic works dealing with general law and with the county and state within which a prospective attorney intended to be licensed. Study in the office of a practicing lawyer was also common. Having thus prepared himself, the applicant arranged to be examined individually by three sitting judges. Upon successful examination, the judges issued to the applicant a license to practice

11. Ibid., entries for 23, 29 May and 18 June 1859.

12. Ibid., entry for 24 May 1859.

13. Ibid., entry for 27 May 1859.

law. The amount of time involved depended, of course, on the ability of the law student and on how much time was available for reading, practice in legal writing, and attendance at court sessions as an observer.

Throughout his time teaching school in Amherst County, Peticolas studied diligently. Typically, he would arise early, read law until his students arrived, then read more after his evening meal. Sundays saw him similarly involved after church, and certainly most of his spare time was spent in studying.[14] His plan was to have Uncle Robert obtain for him a certificate from the court during its May 1859 term, which would attest to his good character, age, and residence. With such a certificate, Peticolas could prepare for and request examination by two judges in Lynchburg and a third judge from nearby Bedford County. When Robert Brown obtained such a certificate for him, Peticolas intensified his study efforts in preparation for the three law exams, and that study preoccupied him for most of the rest of his time in Virginia.[15]

Luckily for Peticolas's concentration, there were very few things for a young man to do in rural Amherst County during 1858 and 1859. Many historians of the era have commented on how boring everyday country life was during the pre–Civil War era, and consequently, how attractive the prospects of war and travel were to many young men of that period. Certainly, Peticolas's prewar journal supports those views. For him, the week's highlight often was seeing a few acquaintances at church on Sunday and picking cherries or peaches after the services were finished. Some diversion was offered by occasional trips into Lynchburg to pick up books or other items he had ordered. Otherwise, the young teacher's life was quite routine and dull.

Increasingly during 1859, however, another interest vied with the study of law for Peticolas's attention. One of his older students was Miss Rhodie Pettyjohn, who lived with her widowed mother on a nearby farm. He tutored the eighteen-year-old girl in French several evenings each week and quickly became fond of her. Just how fond was a matter to which Alfred gave a great deal of thought. He felt that "she is very affectionate and as perfectly natural and unaffected in her ways as it is possible for anyone to be."[16]

---

14. Ibid., entries for 24 May and 16 July 1859.

15. Ibid., entries for 2, 16 May 1859.

16. Ibid., entry for 4 May 1859.

Rhodie encouraged him, returning his affection to a lesser degree while keeping her options open. After the French lessons, she and Alfred usually played checkers or backgammon, and often she played the piano for him. He accompanied her and her friends to church whenever possible and in general spent as much time with her as he could. He was quite irritated when Rhodie entertained, or was courted by, other local young men, and could not understand how she could be so duplicitous toward him and tolerant of such obvious bumpkins. Despite competition, however, Alfred progressed to the point of actually hugging and kissing Miss Rhodie—several times. That was considered pretty spicy; so much so that in his journal, the young man described such encounters in a homemade code.[17] Happily, the code is easily broken.

Throughout the early summer of 1859, Peticolas examined his feelings toward Rhodie Pettyjohn. He decided he loved her and that she must love him, despite certain indications to the contrary. Accordingly, he proposed marriage to her during June. Miss Rhodie had many objections, however, and gave him no immediate answer. She felt she was too young and wanted to continue her education, although the prospect of marriage was also attractive.[18]

For Alfred, his proposal brought into focus a dilemma. By marrying Miss Rhodie he would gain possession of her property. Her farm was too small to afford more than a modest living, and the prospect of settling into an agrarian life had little appeal. As a farmer, he would have to give up his goal of becoming an attorney, and thus lose his first love—the law. This he seemed reluctant to do. He was not ready to quell his undefined, but increasing, wanderlust; he still wanted to go elsewhere and practice law. Feeling that there was little chance for a young attorney in Amherst County, he talked with others about opportunities outside Virginia. One acquaintance recommended Florida, but Uncle Robert knew of several failures in that frontier state; he felt Peticolas would do much better in the West.[19]

While he tried to resolve the dilemma in his own mind and while Miss Rhodie delayed answering his marriage proposal, Peticolas continued to study law. By mid-June, however, he felt sufficiently prepared to take the first of his examinations. Going into Lynchburg on a Saturday, Peticolas stopped Judge J. P. Marshall

---

17. Ibid., entries for 18, 21 May and 6 July 1859.

18. Ibid., entries for 29 June and 11 July 1859.

19. Ibid., entries for 11, 20, 30 June and 4, 11 July 1859.

after the court session and asked when he might make an appointment to be examined. The judge replied that the present was as good a time as any. Peticolas was "somewhat embarrassed and got into a sort of stupor occasionally . . . , missing two or three questions." For a while he feared the judge would not sign his license, but suddenly the dinner gong sounded, and Judge Marshall asked if Peticolas had his certificate and license. He did, and after obtaining the judge's signature and admonition to read industriously, Alfred left in high spirits.[20]

Peticolas repeated the process the following week before Judge W. B. Daniel in Lynchburg. Expecting a "close examination," he approached the judge's house with "a mingling of dread and confidence." He was again successful after Judge Daniel said, "You have not read as extensive a course as you might have done, but your examination has showed that you have read thoroughly. . . ."[21] Subsequently, he passed a third examination before Judge L. P. Thompson, and on 24 August 1859, the judges of the County Court of Amherst "being satisfied of his qualifications, do hereby license the said Alfred B. Peticolas to practice law in the superior and inferior Courts of this Commonwealth."[22]

With his license in hand, much of Peticolas's problem concerning his future was resolved. Whether Miss Rhodie finally refused his marriage proposal or whether he assumed she had, we do not know, since his only surviving prewar journal ends without answering the question. Whatever the circumstances, the young lawyer decided that he would follow Uncle Robert's advice and move to the West. That he did, settling in the little town of Victoria, Texas, some one hundred miles southeast of San Antonio, during October 1859. After being licensed to practice law in Texas, Peticolas entered into a partnership with Samuel A. White, a prominent Victoria attorney and judge, and editor of the *Victoria Advocate*.[23]

During the immediate pre–Civil War years, while the voices of

20. Ibid., entry for 4 June 1859.

21. Ibid., entry for 11 June 1859.

22. License to Practice, A. B. Peticolas, Amherst County Court, Virginia, 24 August 1859. Original in Local History Collection, Victoria College, Victoria, Texas. Copy in editor's collection.

23. Robert W. Shook, "A. B. Peticolas: 19th Century Victoria Artist," *Victoria College Kaleidoscope* (Spring 1979), 10–12; Family Group Record, A. B. Peticolas and M. G. Peticolas. This information was furnished by Marian H. Martin, Azle, Texas. Copy in editor's collection.

sectionalism became increasingly strident, Peticolas kept his law office and living quarters on the east side of Victoria's Main Street. In addition to practicing law, the new Texan found time to continue his pastime of sketching. His views of the farms and houses in the countryside around Victoria, and of landmarks in the town itself, are about the only remaining visual records of prewar Victoria County.[24]

Peticolas also made many friends in Victoria besides those contacted through his law practice. Several older ladies, some with eligible daughters, befriended the young bachelor. Among these, he counted Mrs. John Shirkey, who managed the Shirkey House, a well-known local hotel that had hosted Col. Robert E. Lee during his tenure in Texas.[25] In addition, Peticolas had several favorites among the young ladies of Victoria. Later, when he was destitute in Franklin (El Paso), Texas, following the New Mexico campaign, Alfred received clothing packages from no fewer than five of these aspirants. There is no indication that he was nearly as fond of any of these women as he had been of Rhodie Pettyjohn, but he married two of them during postwar years.[26]

These peaceful pursuits lasted little more than a year. On 28 January 1861, a secession convention met in Austin. To no one's surprise, it passed an ordinance which, when ratified by the voters, made Texas the seventh state to leave the Federal Union. A martial spirit immediately stirred not only many state politicians, but many young Texans as well. Their initial actions had a direct effect on Peticolas's Civil War career.

Soon after Texas seceded, the Union departmental commander, Gen. David E. Twiggs, surrendered all Federal military property to the state and ordered all his troops to withdraw to the coast and leave Texas. By the end of March, the garrison of Fort Bliss, near Franklin, Texas, had abandoned it to Texas state agents. Subsequently, the soldiers at the other far-western posts—Forts Quitman, Davis, Stockton, Duncan, Lancaster, Hudson, and Clark—did likewise.[27]

---

24. Shook, "A. B. Peticolas," pp. 10–12.

25. Ibid.

26. The women were Mary Dunbar and Marion Goodwin.

27. For a full treatment of the initial Confederate activities in Texas, as well as the subsequent New Mexico campaign, see Martin H. Hall, *Sibley's New Mexico Campaign* (Austin: University of Texas Press, 1960). See also Theophilus Noel, *A Campaign from Santa Fe to the Mississippi: Being a History of the Old Sibley Brigade* . . . (1865; reprint ed., Houston: Stagecoach Press, 1961). Noel was a private in Co. A, Fourth Texas Mounted Volunteers.

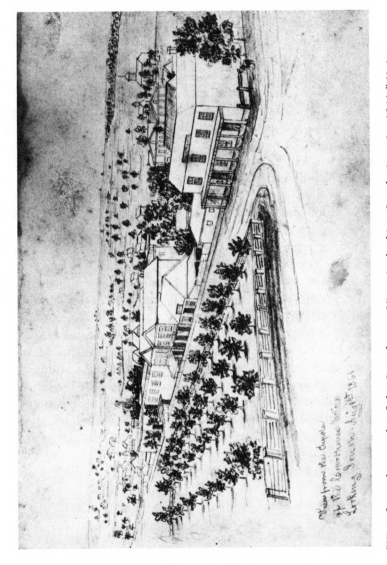

"View from the cupola of the Courthouse, Victoria, looking South, Aug. 1st 1861." (Arizona Historical Society)

With Federal forces gone, Confederate officials decided that the western forts should be regarrisoned to provide protection against increasing Indian raids against the sparse population of West Texas. The Rebels also cast covetous eyes on their huge neighbor to the northwest, New Mexico Territory. Also sparsely populated, that territory comprised the present states of New Mexico and Arizona. The northern part of the region, containing the bulk of the population, the capitol (Santa Fe), the major military posts, and tied to the North through its supply and trade routes, generally favored the Union. The dry, semidesert, lower half of the territory, roughly the area south of the thirty-fourth degree of latitude, was commonly called Arizona, and had few residents indeed. However, those residents heavily favored the Confederacy, since they were tied closely to Texas and the South by birth and by trade interests. During the early months of 1861, the citizens of the Mesilla Valley and the nearby Pinos Altos mining district, as well as those in faraway Tucson, ratified resolutions favoring the Southern Confederacy and seeking its protection under territorial status.[28]

While these resolutions had no legal standing, the Confederate commander in Texas acted on the sentiments indicated and upon the need to reoccupy far West Texas. He dispatched to Fort Bliss approximately 630 men of the Second Regiment of Texas Mounted Rifles, and an attached artillery battery, all under Lt. Col. John R. Baylor.[29] During July 1961, Baylor, with half his command, attacked the nearest Federal outpost, Fort Fillmore, located in the Mesilla Valley some forty miles north of Fort Bliss, near present-day Las Cruces, New Mexico. By audacious maneuver, and aided by almost incredible incompetence on the part of the Union commander of Fort Fillmore, the Texans occupied the abandoned and burned post and subsequently captured its garrison. Following that action, Baylor formed the Confederate Territory of Arizona, with its capitol at Mesilla and with himself as military governor.[30]

---

28. Hall, *Sibley's New Mexico Campaign*, pp. 6–13, 17–18.

29. Present-day El Paso, Texas. The town was known as Franklin until 1873. During the Civil War, the Mexican village across the Rio Grande from Franklin was known as El Paso, or El Paso del Norte, and is now Ciudad Juarez.

30. Hall, *Sibley's New Mexico Campaign*, pp. 25–28; Martin H. Hall, *The Confederate Army of New Mexico* (Austin: Presidial Press, 1978), pp. 18–21; *The War of the Rebellion: A Compilation of the Official Records of the Union and Confederate Armies*, 128 vols. (Washington, D.C., 1880–1901), Series I, vol. IV: 4–7, 16–21. Hereafter cited as *O.R.*, with all citations to Series I.

New Mexico Territory
1861

He and his troops thereafter skirmished with Indians who raided the region around Franklin and into the Mesilla Valley. They also engaged small parties of Union soldiers sent out from Fort Craig, the principal Federal post guarding central New Mexico, on the Rio Grande some 100 miles upriver from Fort Fillmore. The Union departmental commander, Col. Edward R. S. Canby, maintained small outposts at strategic points between Fort Craig and the Texans, and kept patrols in the field to detect any further advance by Baylor.[31]

While the troopers of the Second Texas Mounted Rifles were thus engaged in the Far West, other young men flocked to the colors in South Texas. Well-known and often popular community leaders, many of them local politicians, raised companies of volunteers in the towns and counties of that region. By May 1861, recruiting was under way and generally met with enthusiastic success. In Victoria, the county sheriff, George J. Hampton, a former Ranger, began recruiting a company known as the "Victoria Blues." The job was complete before the end of May, and as was the policy throughout the Confederate army, the men elected their own commissioned and noncommissioned officers. They elected Hampton captain, as might be expected, and they elected the newly enlisted A. B. Peticolas as their Fifth Sergeant, a significant distinction considering his fairly recent arrival in Victoria.[32]

If there was action on the western frontier, however, there was little or none in South Texas. The volunteer companies mustered to learn the fundamentals of soldiering but were soon disillusioned. The relationships between the state and Confederate governments were as yet unclear, and their respective officials were unsure just where the many responsibilities connected with training, supplying, and equipping large numbers of soldiers lay. As a result, the eager recruits were left to find adequate food and shelter in their improvised camps. With little official direction, the company officers were often unable to find employment for their men, or to train or arm them. Dissatisfaction naturally resulted, and to make matters worse, the late spring and summer of 1861 were unusually wet. Rain fell almost continually in South Texas, adding to the soldiers' discomfort. By June, many of the companies simply disbanded, with members returning to their homes and civilian employments, while other

31. *O.R.* IV: 25–32, 40–42, 80–81.

32. Compiled Service Record, A. B. Peticolas, War Department Collection of Confederate Records, Card No. 50741782, Record Group (RG) 109, National Archives (NA).

Brig. Gen. Henry Hopkins Sibley, C. S. A.
(National Archives)

units retained their organization and kept up semiweekly drill schedules.[33]

This picture of military confusion and disenchantment soon changed, however, and the main agent of that change was Henry H. Sibley. A former United States Dragoon officer serving in New Mexico, Sibley had resigned his commission and traveled to Richmond, Virginia, to tender his services to the Confederacy. He had specific services in mind; to President Jefferson Davis, Sibley proposed a plan to conquer New Mexico Territory. He would raise a mounted force in Texas, essentially live off the land en route to and in New Mexico, easily defeat the meager Union forces there, and secure the military supplies, and perhaps natural resources, of the territory.[34]

The scheme sounded farfetched, but the potential rewards were

33. W. R. Howell, "Journal of a Soldier of the Confederate States Army," MSS, Archives Division, Texas State Library, Austin, Texas, entries for 30 April–10 June 1861. A typescript of this journal was prepared by Dr. Philip L. Mead of Albuquerque, and generously shared with the editor. Hereafter cited as Howell Journal. Howell was a private in Co. C, Fifth Texas Mounted Volunteers.

34. Hall, *Confederate Army of New Mexico*, pp. 13–14.

great compared to the small cost of the expedition to the Confederate treasury. Consequently, Jefferson Davis authorized the campaign and commissioned Sibley a brigadier general in the Confederate army. Sibley, however, appears to have had far greater plans for his brigade and campaign than he divulged to Davis. According to his trusted artillery chief, Trevanion T. Teel, the new general planned to enlist large numbers of native New Mexicans to augment his Texans. After defeating the Regular United States forces in New Mexico and capturing Fort Union, the military supply center in the northern part of the territory, Sibley would continue on to capture the rich mining districts around Denver City, Colorado Territory. Upon securing that wealth for the Confederacy, the Rebels would turn westward and be welcomed by the disaffected Mormons of Utah. With his ranks thus swelled, Sibley then apparently planned to march to southern California, capturing there the mines of the region and securing warm-water ports on the Pacific.[35] Even the most optimistic among Sibley's confidants must have seen this strategy as visionary in the extreme.

There were numerous flaws in Sibley's plan. As an experienced serving officer in New Mexico, he should have known that the Hispanic natives would be unlikely to join his forces. The majority of these people had no great interest in or affection for the federal government, but the powerful native merchants and Anglo officials did. More important, however, the native people detested Texans.[36] Furthermore, the Rio Grande Valley would barely support its indigenous population, much less 3,000 additional mounted soldiers. It was not possible for a brigade to live off the land in New Mexico. In addition, the Federal forces were, with few exceptions, competently led and staunchly Unionist. In Colorado, the miners tended also to be fiercely loyal to the old flag, while there is no evidence that the Utah Mormons, who undoubtedly cared little for the federal government, had any affection for or seriously considered alliance with the Confederates. Similarly, while a few vocal Southern sympathizers in California attracted attention early in 1861, the major-

---

35. Trevanion T. Teel, "Sibley's New Mexico Campaign: Its Objects and the Causes of Its Failure," *Battles and Leaders of the Civil War,* 4 vols. (1884–88; reprint ed., New York: Yoseloff, 1956), 2: 700.

36. For a detailed study of native New Mexican attitudes and service during the Sibley campaign, see Darlis A. Miller, "Hispanos and the Civil War in New Mexico: A Reconsideration," *New Mexico Historical Review* 54 (April 1979): 105–23.

ity of that state's people were loyal, and in fact rapidly organized military forces to oppose Sibley.

The scheme was simply impossible given the logistics and communications of the time, but even if it had been practical, there was a final flaw. Sibley himself was not the man for the job. A reasonably good organizer, he was a heavy drinker, being described as a "walking whiskey keg."[37] In addition, his courage was suspect; somehow, he managed to miss every battle fought during the New Mexico campaign.

These flaws of planning and character later coalesced to disillusion his soldiers, but in the high summer of 1861 they were not apparent, and Sibley's arrival in San Antonio on 12 August sparked an enthusiasm in the dormant Texas volunteers which equaled that experienced earlier in the year. The new general planned to raise a brigade of approximately 3,000 mounted men for his upcoming campaign. Recruiting began immediately, but despite the rush to arms, competition with other regiments organizing for service in the East delayed Sibley's plans. Full strength for each of the three regiments comprising the brigade was approximately 1,000 men, and finding that number of soldiers who could provide their own horses, horse equipment, and arms was more difficult than he imagined.[38]

In Victoria, Hampton's unemployed company of volunteers quickly signed up for service in the Sibley Brigade. They retained their previous organization, but now styled themselves the "Victoria Invincibles." A. B. Peticolas enrolled with his company on 22 August 1861. After settling his personal affairs in Victoria, Peticolas marched for San Antonio, and in that city, on 11 September, he was mustered into Confederate service for the duration of the war. The twenty-three-year-old trooper brought with him a horse valued at $110 and equipment worth $15, as appraised by the Confederate authorities.[39] As the third company to join the Sibley Brigade, Peticolas's unit became Company C, Fourth Regiment of Texas Mounted Volunteers.

Shortly thereafter, Captain Hampton led the men eastward out of San Antonio to their camp of instruction located on Salado Creek, along the road to Austin. Camp Sibley, as the men of the Fourth Texas soon christened the place, was well chosen and provided "a

---

37. Hall, *Sibley's New Mexico Campaign*, p. 54.

38. Hall, *Confederate Army of New Mexico*, p. 15.

39. Compiled Service Record, A. B. Peticolas, War Department Collection of Confederate Records, Cards No. 50235511 and 50235413, RG 109, NA.

beautiful drill ground," according to one of Peticolas's companions.[40] For a month, the members of Company C learned the fundamentals of military life, including drill movements, guard mounting, and disciplinary requirements. How disciplined each company became was a function of the inclinations and abilities of the company officers, and to some extent of the men themselves. Those factors varied widely within the regiment and within the brigade. Although there were "wild boys" enrolled, the majority of Sibley's men appear to have been of excellent character, many well educated, and generally inspired by the enthusiastic patriotism seen in early war enlistees throughout the North and South. The widely held picture of these Texans as a rowdy, undisciplined crowd seems to have come more from their own accounts of their individualistic, open-order tactics in battle rather than from any unusually licentious behavior away from the battlefield.[41]

By 20 September, the Fourth Texas was completely recruited and was under the command of Col. James Reily of Houston, a prominent Texas politician and former United States consul in Russia. Reily was an efficient administrator, but took no part in the subsequent fighting in New Mexico, being detached to diplomatic duties in Mexico by General Sibley. Instead, the regiment's battle leader was its lieutenant colonel, William R. Scurry. A renowned veteran of the Mexican War, a lawyer and politician from Clinton, Texas, Scurry won the admiration of his men for his courage and leadership in battle, as well as his concern for their welfare throughout the campaign.[42] Peticolas praised him in his journal as "the best officer, most polished gentleman, most sociable gentleman, and the most popular Colonel in the whole outfit."

With good leaders and good training, the members of Company C were well served. In other areas, however, they were neglected. Their clothing was often civilian apparel worn from home, sometimes being fashioned by a mother or sister in "military style." In other cases, Federal uniforms, acquired by the surrender of United

---

40. David B. Gracy, II, ed., "New Mexico Campaign Letters of Frank Starr, 1861–1862," *Texas Military History* 4 (Fall 1964), 170–71. Hereafter cited as Starr Campaign Letters. Starr served as a private, then first sergeant, of Co. H., Fourth Texas Mounted Volunteers.

41. Noel, *A Campaign from Santa Fe to the Mississippi*, pp. 12–13; Howell Journal, entries for 9–29 September 1861.

42. Hall, *Confederate Army of New Mexico*, pp. 51–54.

Col. James Reily, Lt. Col. William R. Scurry, commanders of the Fourth Texas Mounted Volunteers, C. S. A. (Texas State Library)

States material to Texas authorities, were issued. In addition, Confederate quartermasters may have issued regular gray uniforms, or parts of uniforms, before Sibley's men left for New Mexico, but there is no hard evidence to support this possibility.[43] Company C's arms were equally varied. Each volunteer was required to furnish himself with "a good double barrel shot gun or rifle certain, a bowie knife and six shooter, if the latter can possibly be obtained." As a result, the troopers were equipped with shotguns, sporting rifles, muskets, and military long arms of all sorts, as well as a variety of pistols, by the time they left for New Mexico. One sister unit, Company G, composed largely of German settlers from Austin County, even equipped themselves with "spears" to become one of two such lancer companies in Sibley's brigade. In addition, ordnance officers issued arms confiscated from the Federal armories. Peticolas was apparently the recipient of one of these better firearms, a so-called minie-

43. Howell Journal, entries for 2, 3, May 1861; Walter A. Faulkner, contrib., "With Sibley in New Mexico; the Journal of William Henry Smith," *West Texas Historical Association Year Book* 27 (October 1951): 114. Hereafter cited as Smith Journal. Smith was a private in Co. I, Fifth Texas Mounted Volunteers.

Maj. Trevanion T. Teel, First Texas Artillery. (Editor's Collection)

gun, which was the standard Springfield Model 1855 or 1861 Rifle Musket, of .58 caliber. He also had a bowie knife that he later traded for a two-foot-long sword "of first-rate metal." Somewhere along the way, he also acquired a pistol, as shown in his self-portrait after the campaign. The Texans were frustrated at not being more uniformly armed, but were heartened when each regiment was assigned a battery of four small mountain howitzers, also from surrendered Union stocks.[44]

In addition to Peticolas's regiment, Sibley also organized and recruited the Fifth and Seventh Regiments of Texas Mounted Volunteers. The soldiers universally referred to the Fourth, Fifth, and Seventh Texas Mounted Volunteers as the First, Second, and Third regiments, respectively, of the Sibley Brigade. Peticolas used that terminology throughout his Civil War journal, and to avoid confusion, those designations have been retained. The Third Regiment was not completely filled until mid-November, and the Confederate commander could not wait that long. He was anxious over the ex-

44. *Austin State Gazette*, 7 September 1861; Noel, *A Campaign from Santa Fe to the Mississippi*, p. 13; Oscar Haas, trans., "The Diary of Julius Giesecke, 1861–1862," *Texas Military History* 3 (Winter 1963), entry for 23 December 1861. Hereafter cited as Giesecke Diary. Giesecke served as second lieutenant, then captain, of Co. G, Fourth Texas Mounted Volunteers.

Twelve-pounder mountain howitzer. This was one of the artillery pieces used by the Sibley Brigade in New Mexico and subsequently buried by the Confederates at Albuquerque. Maj. Teel located the guns in 1889, and they were unearthed. The original barrels are on display at the Albuquerque Museum. (Bill Lasker Photo)

posed position of Colonel Baylor's small force holding Fort Bliss and the Mesilla Valley. Consequently, after reviewing the fully organized portion of the brigade during October, he decided to commence active campaigning.[45]

Early on the morning of 22 October 1861, Fifth Sergeant Peticolas was in the saddle and headed for the first great adventures of his Civil War career. Colonel Reily formed the First Regiment for a stirring patriotic speech at Camp Sibley, then, in "column of fours," led them westward to San Antonio, where they formed in solid mass on the main plaza for a second ceremony. Peticolas listened to yet another eloquent speech by Reily and a less impressive address by General Sibley. With three cheers for their commanders, the troopers then filed out of town, marching westward to their first camp, near Leon Creek. There, the weather immediately turned cold, and rain

45. Howell Journal, entries for 6–21 October 1861; Hall, *Confederate Army of New Mexico*, pp. 15, 17.

fell throughout the night, affording the members of Company C their first taste of misery to come.[46]

The journey facing the Texans was daunting. Their path was along the stage road between San Antonio and Fort Bliss, some 630 miles away. As the First Regiment took up the line of march on 26 October, the long column of mounted troopers was accompanied by a beef herd and an extensive wagon train, as well as their attached artillery battery. Supply wagons carried ammunition, medicines, food, forage, and other military equipment, while each company had three additional wagons for the personal belongings of the enlisted men and officers. The command's horses were not overburdened, and Peticolas and his companions could make good time along the first part of their journey. Their route led generally westward from San Antonio, through Castroville and Uvalde to Fort Clark, near Brackettsville. Confederate troops had already garrisoned that post by the time Sibley's men passed it, and on 6 November, two weeks after leaving the cheering crowds in downtown San Antonio, Peticolas reached what many of the men considered the end of civilization, San Felipe Springs, some fifteen miles from the Rio Grande.[47]

While near Fort Clark, Colonel Reily intercepted an urgent message from Colonel Baylor, at Doña Ana in the Mesilla Valley, forecasting an attack by Union forces and asking for reinforcements. With General Sibley still back in San Antonio, Reily decided to hurry his men on toward New Mexico. Since water supplies along the route would be inadequate for the entire First Regiment, Colonel Reily divided his force into three battalions for the rest of the journey westward. Peticolas was in the third battalion, as Company C marched with Companies E, I, and K along the increasingly rough stage road. The Second Regiment and portions of the Third Regiment, similarly subdivided, followed at regular intervals.[48]

From San Felipe Springs, Company C rode northward "through a country where mesquite could not grow, cactus were drying up, and grass and such good things were not to be thought of." However,

---

46. Noel, *A Campaign from Santa Fe to the Mississippi*, pp. 15–16; Giesecke Diary, entries for 23, 24 October 1861.

47. Giesecke Diary, entries for 26 October–6 November 1861; Hall, *Confederate Army of New Mexico*, p. 17.

48. *O.R.* IV: 133; Noel, *A Campaign from Santa Fe to the Mississippi*, p. 16; Giesecke Diary, entry for 7 November 1861.

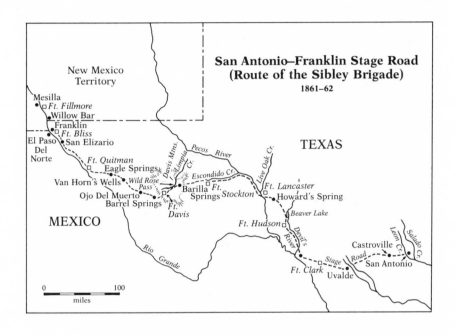

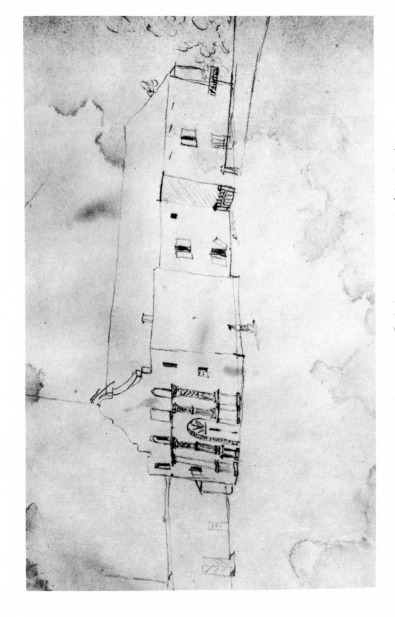

Peticolas's sketch of the Alamo, date unspecified. (Arizona Historical Society)

they soon reached the beautiful Devil's River and continued up that stream for three days, passing the Confederate garrison at Fort Hudson and camping on 14 November at Beaver Lake, near the head of Devil's River, some 246 miles from San Antonio. The stages were still running between Franklin and San Antonio, so Peticolas and his companions were able to send letters back home and receive mail sent forward from Victoria.[49]

From Beaver Lake the stage road led westward to the Pecos River, passing Howard's Spring, where water for the company's horses had to be passed up in buckets from the source some twelve feet below the surface. For Peticolas, the journey was without particular incident, although scarcity of water became increasingly common. On 18 November he camped near Fort Lancaster, on Live Oak Creek, then rode northward along the Pecos River to its junction with Escondido Creek. His route then turned westward to Fort Stockton, a point 400 miles from San Antonio and about 230 miles from Fort Bliss. The season's first frost replaced pleasant autumn weather as Company C continued toward the Davis Mountains in far west Texas. Past the deep water hole at Leon Spring, the road led to the clear Limpia Creek, then along that stream through spectacular Wild Rose Pass. Here Peticolas's battalion caught up with the First Regiment units that had been traveling two days in advance. Together, the Texas horsemen reached Fort Davis on 2 December.[50]

Although Federal troops had been gone from Fort Davis for some time, the post was far from abandoned. Confederate garrison troops, stage company employees, and a post sutler were present. From the latter, some of the troopers obtained liquor and "got tight." As his men passed into and through Fort Davis, Colonel Reily and some of his officers remained behind for some time and "tanked up considerably."[51] Peticolas's third battalion probably remained at the post for a day or two in order to let the second battalion precede them to the few water holes in the western reaches of the Davis Mountains.

---

49. Giesecke Diary, entries for 8–11, 16 November 1861; Howell Journal, entry for 27 November 1861; Smith Journal, p. 118.

50. Giesecke Diary, entries for 12 November–2 December 1861; Howell Journal, entry for 29 November 1861; Smith Journal, p. 118.

51. Giesecke Diary, entry for 2 December 1861; Howell Journal, entry for 15 December 1861.

Peticolas's sketches of the stage station and main buildings of Ft. Hudson, drawn when he passed the former Federal post during July 1862, retracing his westward journey of 1861. (Arizona Historical Society)

26

"View of Ft. Lancaster, July 2nd '62." Abandoned Federal post on the Ft. Bliss–San Antonio stage road. (Arizona Historical Society)

"Fort Davis, Texas, 22nd June 1862." Drawing of the Confederate-occupied post. (Arizona Historical Society)

Although the road so far had not been exceedingly rough, Peticolas's horse had given out on the last day of November. Probably at Fort Davis, he bought a new mount, a riding mule that served him until it was killed at the Battle of Valverde, three months later.[52] Sibley's men were not equipped to fight as cavalry on horseback; rather, they were actually mounted infantry. As such, being mounted on mules, as many were, was no handicap; and in fact that animal's hardiness could be a distinct advantage.

Peticolas rode westward with Company C, camping at Barrel Springs and Ojo del Muerto, or Dead Man's Spring, some twenty-eight miles beyond Fort Davis. The battalions of the First Regiment followed the stage route on to Van Horn's Wells and Eagle Springs, while the following Second Regiment units blazed a new road farther south. Although the scenery was spectacular, wood was as scarce as water during this part of the journey, and Sibley's men were eager to reach the Rio Grande, which promised plenty of both commodities. Peticolas first saw that river, which was to be so familiar to him during the next few months, on 10 December, as his company arrived at a point about seven miles below Fort Quitman.[53]

That wretched post, occupied by about twenty Confederate soldiers, was soon passed as the Texans continued upriver toward Franklin and Fort Bliss. As they did so, General Sibley and his staff caught up with them and went on ahead. Soon thereafter, Peticolas's battalion overtook the preceding units, and on 13 December, the First Regiment was reunited and camped for two days, resting both men and animals. They were only two days away from Franklin, and after passing the river towns of San Elizario and Isleta, reached that long-sought goal, with nearby Fort Bliss, on 17 December 1861.[54]

General Sibley had reached Fort Bliss a few days earlier, and there, on 14 December, he assumed command of "all the forces of the Confederate States on the Rio Grande at and above Fort Quitman and all in the Territory of New Mexico and Arizona." He designated his force the Army of New Mexico, although it was in fact only a brigade-size command.[55] When all its components were concen-

---

52. Compiled Service Record, A. B. Peticolas, War Department Collection of Confederate Records, Card No. 50235555, RG 109, NA.

53. Giesecke Diary, entries for 2–8 December 1861.

54. Ibid., entries for 7–17 December 1861; Herbert M. Hart, *Old Forts of the Southwest* (Seattle: Superior Publishing Co., 1964), pp. 130–31.

55. *O.R.* IV: 157–58.

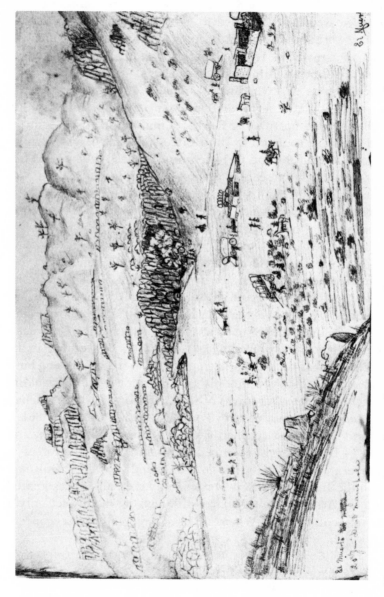

Texan camp at spring and ruined stage station at El Muerto, or Ojo de Muerto, west of Fort Davis, Texas. (Arizona Historical Society)

trated, Sibley would lead approximately 3,200 men of the First, Second, and Third regiments, as well as Baylor's soldiers, who had come out the preceding summer, and locally recruited volunteers including a company of "Santa Fe gamblers" known rather accurately as the Brigands.[56]

Still worried about the exposed nature of Baylor's positions in the Mesilla Valley, Sibley sent the First Regiment northward without delay. Peticolas camped only one night near Fort Bliss, then continued up the Rio Grande. Along that river, Company C began to face another enemy in addition to the anticipated Federal troops and the increasingly cold weather. Indians raided their horse herd at night, running off a number of badly needed mounts. By 20 December, the First Regiment had reached Willow Bar, a well-known camping spot some twenty-five miles north of Fort Bliss. There, the troopers stayed for a week, holding regular drill sessions, replacing the lancer company's useless weapons with guns, spending a lonely Christmas in a strange and remote land, and experiencing their first New Mexico dust storm, "so thick that it is impossible to see a horse fifty yards away," on the day after Christmas. There also, Colonel Reily left for detached duty, and command of the First Regiment devolved upon Lieutenant Colonel Scurry.[57]

After moving their camp downriver a couple of miles for better grazing, the men of the First Regiment quickly began to tire of the inactivity, broken only by drill and such chores as washing clothes in the cold, muddy waters of the Rio Grande. Finally, on 3 January 1862, they received orders to move northward once again. Peticolas rode past Fort Fillmore, abandoned by the Federals the previous summer, past Mesilla, capitol of Confederate Arizona Territory, and through the villages of Las Cruces and Doña Ana. Preceded by two of the local "spy companies," he and Company C crossed the river for the first time, and on 8 January, had reached camp two and one-half miles above Fort Thorn, a frontier post abandoned three years previously.[58] Here they were some seventy miles from their enemies at Fort Craig.

While General Sibley supplanted Colonel Baylor in command of the advanced Confederate forces in the Mesilla Valley and planned his movement still farther into New Mexico, the fretting troopers of

56. Hall, *Confederate Army of New Mexico*, pp. 23, 373–76.

57. Ibid., p. 23; Giesecke Diary, entries for 17–27 December 1861.

58. Giesecke Diary, entries for 28 December 1861–8 January 1862.

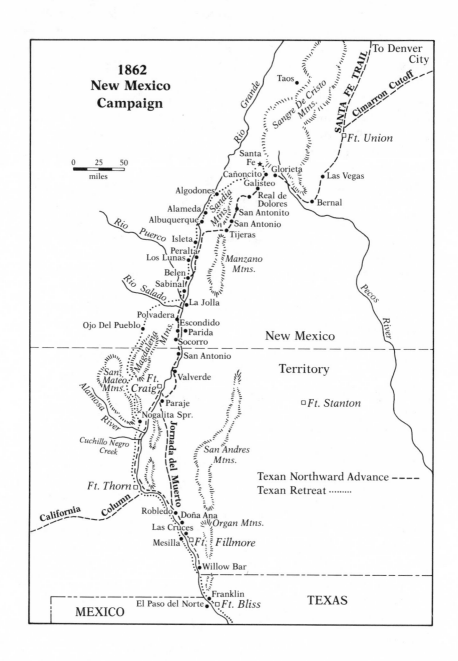

**1862
New Mexico
Campaign**

0   25   50
miles

To Denver
City

Rio Grande

Taos

Sangre De Cristo Mtns.

SANTA FE TRAIL

Cimarron Cutoff

Ft. Union

Santa Fe

Cañoncito   Glorieta

Galisteo   Las Vegas

Algodones   Real de Dolores

Alameda   San Antonito   Bernal

Albuquerque   Sandia Mtns.   San Antonio

Isleta   Tijeras

Peralta

Los Lunas

Belen   Manzano Mtns.

Sabinal

Rio Puerco

Rio Salado

La Jolla

Polvadera

Ojo Del Pueblo   Escondido

Parida

Socorro

New Mexico

Pecos River

San Antonio

Territory

Magdalena Mtns.

San Mateo Mtns.   Ft. Craig   Valverde

Ft. Stanton

Alamosa River   Paraje

Nogalita Spr.

Cuchillo Negro Creek

Jornada del Muerto

San Andres Mtns.

Texan Northward Advance ----
Texan Retreat ....

Ft. Thorn

California   Column

Robledo   Doña Ana

Las Cruces   Organ Mtns.

Mesilla   Ft. Fillmore

Willow Bar

Franklin

MEXICO   El Paso del Norte   Ft. Bliss   TEXAS

32

Company C spent over a month in the vicinity of Fort Thorn. Camp routine quickly became boring, with few incidents to enliven their days. Indians continued sporadic night raids on the horses, and Peticolas accompanied one expedition by his company and Company G that chased a band of marauders north along the Rio Grande, then up a side canyon on Cuchillo Negro Creek. That pursuit was as fruitless as most, and he once again settled down to routine drills, guard duty, and boredom. Many members of the regiment became increasingly restless, and with the sutlers having caught up with the soldiers, drinking began to be a serious problem in camp. To add to the soldiers' unrest, light snow fell, the weather became very cold, and sickness became more prevalent.[59]

Hopes for a rapid advance northward rose as elements of the Second Regiment arrived on 15 January and, with six companies of Baylor's command, under Maj. Charles L. Pyron, went into camp nearby. No immediate movement was forthcoming, however, and as Sibley dawdled near Fort Thorn, his men and horses continued to eat, soon almost depleting the meager rations and fodder on hand. These hard times were punctuated, though not relieved, by arrival of mail from home during late January, the last Peticolas would see for three months, and by religious services on Sundays.[60]

Finally, the remaining units of Sibley's invasion force arrived at Fort Thorn, and the general was ready to move. On 7 February, Lt. Col. John S. Sutton brought five companies of the Third Regiment into camp. Sibley thereupon issued orders for the advance toward Fort Craig. His force comprised about 2,500 mounted men, with fifteen pieces of artillery and an extensive supply train.[61] This time Peticolas's unit was not in the lead. That honor went to the Second Regiment, accompanied by Captain Teel's Battery B of the First Texas Artillery. Leaving behind large numbers of sick men suffering and dying from smallpox and pneumonia, the Texans broke camp on the same day Sutton arrived. They rode along the Rio Grande toward what they, and Sibley, thought would be an easy occupation of Fort Craig, and after that, Fort Union and the whole of New Mexico Territory.[62]

---

59. Ibid., entries for 9 January–2 February 1862.

60. Ibid., entry for 27 January 1862; Howell Journal, entries for 15, 17 January 1862; Smith Journal, p. 127.

61. Hall, *Confederate Army of New Mexico*, pp. 23–25.

62. Howell Journal, entry for 7 February 1862; Smith Journal, p. 129.

Maj. Gen. E. R. S. Canby. As a colonel,
then brigadier general, he commanded
the Department of New Mexico and led
the Federal defense against the Texan
invasion. (National Archives)

While the Confederates spent an inordinate amount of time organizing, then sluggishly advanced toward him, the Federal commander, Colonel Canby, was extremely active. Once he was convinced the Confederates intended to attack him up the Rio Grande Valley, rather than along the Pecos River, Canby concentrated his forces. He called in garrisons from far-flung outposts, reinforced the walls and other defenses of Fort Craig, activated the territory's volunteer and militia units, and brought an adequate supply of ammunition and food down from Albuquerque and Fort Union.[63] He also re-

63. *O.R.* IV: 78–80; Joseph M. Bell, "The Campaign of New Mexico, 1862." *War Papers Read Before the Commandery of the State of Wisconsin, Military Order of the Loyal Legion of the United States* (Milwaukee, 1891), 1: 51; Nolie Mumey, ed., *Bloody Trails Along the Rio Grande: The Diary of A. F. Ickis* (Denver, Fred A. Rosenstock, 1958), entry for 15 February 1862. Hereafter cited as Ickis Diary. Bell was a first lieutenant in the Third U.S. Cavalry and served in McRae's Battery at Valverde. Ickis was a private in Dodd's Independent Company of Colorado Volunteers.

quested that the governor of Colorado Territory send "as large a force of the Colorado volunteers as can possibly be spared." That request was promptly met, and elements of the "Pikes Peakers" prepared for their key roles in the battles to come.[64]

By mid-February, Canby had approximately 3,800 men available in and around Fort Craig. Of that number, however, only 1,200 were seasoned and trained regulars. The only complete and reasonably well-trained local unit present was Col. Christopher "Kit" Carson's First New Mexico Volunteer regiment of almost 1,000 men. Companies from the Second, Third, Fourth, and Fifth New Mexico Volunteers, and hastily collected, raw militia made up the balance, along with the first of the Colorado troops to arrive, Capt. Theodore H. Dodd's Independent Company, which had made a strenuous forced march to join Canby. With this mixture of veteran and untrained troops, the Union commander awaited the oncoming Texans.[65]

Sibley planned to march his men northward in detachments, then concentrate for an assault on Fort Craig. Consequently, A. B. Peticolas was in the saddle and riding with the First Regiment on 10 February, three days behind the advance element of the brigade. Members of Company C were hungry and cold as they passed up the Rio Grande Valley, surrounded by distant mountain ranges white from recent snowstorms. Their supply wagons caught up with the horsemen that night, and Peticolas's friend Ebenezer Hanna claimed that "we have enough to eat now for the first time since we left San Antonio."[66]

Four days later, the First Regiment reached a point some forty miles below Fort Craig, near the mouth of the Alamosa River. Just as they settled into camp for the night, urgent word arrived from the advance party that Col. Thomas "Tom" Green, the Second Regiment's commander, already near the fort, expected to be attacked

---

64. *O.R.* IV: 82. For the role played by Colorado troops during the Sibley campaign, see William C. Whitford, *Colorado Volunteers in the Civil War, The New Mexico Campaign in 1862* (1906; reprint ed., Boulder, Colo., Pruett Press, 1963). See also Ovando J. Hollister, *Boldly They Rode* (1863; reprint ed., Lakewood, Colo., Golden Press, 1949). Hollister was a private in Co. F, First Colorado Volunteers.

65. Bell, "The Campaign of New Mexico," pp. 52–54; Hall, *Sibley's New Mexico Campaign*, p. 73.

66. Ebenezer Hanna, "The Journal of Ebenezer Hanna," MSS, Archives Division, Texas State Library, Austin, Texas, entry for 10 February 1862. Hereafter cited as Hanna Journal. Hanna was a private in Co. C, Fourth Texas Mounted Volunteers and was killed at Glorieta.

by the enemy. At midnight the bugles sounded, and Peticolas and his companions saddled their horses and mules and once again headed north. The thirty-five-mile forced march was the most arduous they had yet faced. A new storm blew sleet and snow at them "so hard as to almost pelt the skin off our faces."[67] They arrived by eight o'clock, joining the Second and Third regiments and Pyron's battalion from Baylor's command. With their forces thus concentrated, the Texans looked forward to confronting their enemies, but they got little action. After skirmishing briefly with outlying pickets from Fort Craig, the Confederates returned to their camps, some twelve miles south of the post. The snowstorm struck again during the evening, and Peticolas spent a miserable night sleeping on the ground without food or blankets, since the company's wagons had not caught up with the mounted troopers.[68]

On the following day, Company C remained in camp while the rest of Sibley's brigade advanced to within sight of Fort Craig. The post appeared too strong to attack with the force available, so, on 16 February, under Colonel Green's command, the Texans advanced in line of battle, hoping to entice Canby out onto the open plain south of the fort for a decisive fight. With artillery covering their left flank and the Rio Grande bottomland their right, the Rebels had a strong position, made even stronger when the First Regiment rode up to join the line during early afternoon. Canby refused the bait, but as the Texans began to withdraw, he led a small cavalry force out to cut off any stragglers. These Federals exchanged shots with the departing Confederates, and while the action did not amount to much, Peticolas and the men of Company C, on the left of the battle line, for the first time experienced the sensation of shooting at their enemies and hearing bullets whistle by in return. By nightfall of 16 February, they had returned to camps strung out along the road approximately four to six miles south of Fort Craig.[69]

From the roof of the post sutler's store, Union observers could, for the next two days, see "the parks of artillery, towns of shelter tents, grazing horses, lounging men, curling smoke, all framed within

67. Hanna Journal, entries for 13, 14 February 1862.

68. Ibid., 14 February 1862; Giesecke Diary, entry for 14 February 1862; Howell Journal, entry for 14 February 1862; Ickis Diary, entry for 14 February 1862.

69. Hanna Journal, entry for 16 February 1862; Giesecke Diary, entry for 16 February 1862; Howell Journal, entry for 16 February 1862.

Col. Thomas Green, Fifth Texas
Mounted Volunteers, C. S. A.
(Editor's Collection)

the disc of field glasses."[70] Blowing sand replaced the snowstorm as
Sibley and his officers decided on their next move.

The Confederate leaders were faced with a dilemma. In their
front lay an apparently impregnable fort with a resolute garrison
reinforced by large numbers of volunteer soldiers camped outside
the walls. Behind lay the Mesilla Valley–Fort Bliss region, already
stripped of provisions. With only a ten-day supply of food remaining,
some decisive move was obviously needed. General Sibley being
stricken by an unidentified illness as well as by indecision, Colonel
Green decided on one more attempt to draw Canby's forces out of
their fortress into open battle. The Texans would bypass Fort Craig
to the east, passing behind the high, flat-topped volcanic Mesa de
la Contadera (known as Black Mesa or "table mountain" to Peticolas
and his companions) across the Rio Grande from the post. They
would then return to the river near Valverde, six miles north of the

70. Bell, "The Campaign of New Mexico," p. 57.

fort, and a well-known camping place along the road leading on to Albuquerque and Santa Fe. With his lines of supply thus threatened, Canby would have little choice but to leave Fort Craig and fight the Texans on ground chosen by themselves. It was a fairly desperate plan, since the Federal forces would control Sibley's supply line if they were not decisively beaten and the fort captured. Nevertheless, it was probably the best plan that could have been devised under the circumstances, and it dictated the movements of the Sibley Brigade for the next few days.[71]

Early in the morning of 19 February, Peticolas was again in the saddle as the brigade slowly crossed the icy Rio Grande below Fort Craig and marched eastward about three miles to camp near the tiny village of Paraje. There they were near enough to the river to water their mounts, the accompanying supply-train animals, and the beef herd being driven along behind the train.[72]

Canby sent no forces to oppose the river crossing and only offered token resistance during the following day. However, 20 February was a day to be remembered by Peticolas and the men of the First Regiment; it was a day of excitement as well as almost unrelieved toil. Terrain was the main enemy rather than the Federals. There are two major elevations east of the Rio Grande opposite Fort Craig. The lower is a wide shelf of volcanic rock, sandy in places, some 100 feet above the riverbed and near enough to put the post within range of artillery placed along its rimrocks. This lower shelf extends southward from Black Mesa toward Paraje and the Texan campsites. Approximately two miles farther east from the river lies the higher elevation, actually the edge of a vast plain, level with the top of "table mountain." Parallel sandy ridges and ravines connect the lower shelf with the higher elevation.

Peticolas left the Paraje camp early in the morning as part of the long Confederate column. The first part of the day's march was not difficult, as the Texans rode northward along the lower shelf, parallel with the river. However, to keep out of sight of Fort Craig, and to reach the higher elevation where they could pass around Black Mesa, Sibley's men veered away from the river, up a broad ravine. Almost a mile in length, the ravine is composed of apparently bottomless sand. The climb was very difficult for the mounted troopers, but by

71. *O.R.* IV: 507; Hall, *Sibley's New Mexico Campaign*, pp. 78–79.

72. Howell Journal, entry for 19 February 1862; Hanna Journal, entry for 19 February 1862.

late afternoon the advance had reached the top. For wheeled vehicles, however, the route, which had appeared easy from below, was almost impossible. Many thin-tired artillery pieces and the heavily laden wagons sank up to their hubs. Drivers double- and triple-teamed their stuck vehicles. Troopers dismounted to heave on wheels and wagon beds, and together men and animals struggled throughout the day and until well after dark to force the supply train up the long slope to the head of the ravine. There, some five miles from Fort Craig, the exhausted men made a dry camp in an extensive mesquite grove, using that meager wood supply for their cooking fires and the last water in their canteens for their immediate relief.[73]

While the teamsters and most of Sibley's soldiers thus struggled with the wagons, members of the advance guard, and other Texans reaching the top before dark, had a livelier time. During the afternoon, Canby sent a small force of cavalry, infantry, and artillery out from Fort Craig to harass the Confederates' march. These Federals were also much impeded by the deep sand, then advanced toward the Texans, who could be seen on the skyline above them.[74] Observing this intriguing display, the Confederates established their own defensive line along a ridge running westward from their camp. Captain Teel's artillery, the First Regiment's battery of mountain howitzers, and the accompanying brass band joined the dismounted troopers. Company C watched as the band struck up "Dixie," and when the Union troops were within a half-mile of their position, the Texan cannons fired. Although only one casualty resulted from this barrage, some of the inexperienced New Mexico Volunteers were terrified by the noise and exploding shells and could not be kept in line. As a result, Canby withdrew the force back into Fort Craig, leaving an infantry picket line east of the river to deny use of the lower, commanding shelf to the enemy's artillery. The Texans cheered with every shot fired at the confused Unionists, then retired to their own camp.[75]

---

73. *O.R.*, Atlas: Plate XII. This camp of the Fourth Texas was located in 1978 as a result of extensive research by Dee D. Brecheisen of Bosque Farms, New Mexico. Identification of nearby camps and wagon parks was subsequently made through artifact evidence by him, the editor, and Dr. Philip L. Mead of Albuquerque. Mr. Brecheisen generously shared the result of his research and work with the editor.

74. Bell, "The Campaign of New Mexico," pp. 58–59; Hall, *Sibley's New Mexico Campaign*, p. 80.

75. Starr Campaign Letters, p. 172; Ickis Diary, entry for 20 February 1862. The Federal line was located in 1982 by Raymond Scott and Jacob Johnson, of Albuquerque. They generously shared that information with the editor.

With the excitement over, Peticolas and the other members of the "Victoria Invincibles" made their preparations for the severe encounter that all believed would take place the next day. Around little fires built just below the brow of the ridge, out of sight of Fort Craig, they talked and cast bullets from lead bars melted over the glowing coals. Some replaced missing or defective shoes on their mounts, while others made a miserable meal in the dry camp. The river at Valverde still lay five miles ahead, but it offered the prospect of water and action, so the thoughts of those desirable commodities mixed with prebattle apprehension in the soldiers' minds. Other thoughts would soon concern them. In the dark surrounding the camp, the First Regiment's horse herders were careless, and approximately 150 mules used to pull their supply and baggage wagons ran off toward the Rio Grande seeking water.[76]

As the morning of 21 February broke, and this loss was discovered, Lieutenant Colonel Scurry ordered some wagons lightened and others abandoned and burned. That accomplished, A. B. Peticolas rode away from the wretched camp toward the first and largest battle in New Mexico. Thus, with the young soldier approaching the Battle of Valverde, his Civil War journal begins.

---

76. Starr Campaign Letters, p. 172.

The Journal of A. B. Peticolas

Friday, 21 February 1862

This morning at an early hour we got into line and formed to cover the advance of the wagons. Water was extremely scarce; dried beef our only breakfast. We found that about all of the mules of the 1st Regiment were gone this morning, and after the trains had taken up the line of march this morning, the wagons without teams were burned to keep them from falling into the hands of the enemy.[1] A detachment of men was sent down to the river to guard the water, and in about an hour after we had gotten under way, news came back to us that Baylor's command,[2] who had gone down to the river, had engaged the enemy, who were appearing in large numbers. Upon receipt of this intelligence we struck a brisk trot and rode rapidly over the high table land and down a long slant to the river bottom, which is very broad here. When we had gotten nearly to the bottom we heard the discharges of cannon, and I saw a man on the high

---

1. Apparently this destruction was incomplete. Major Charles E. Wesche, Second New Mexico Militia, reported that during the afternoon he and a force of 200 men located "an abandoned camp, formed of partially loaded wagons." The Federal militiamen blew up and burned the entire train. The site was located and identified in 1978, as previously noted. (*O.R.* LIII: 452–53.)

2. Peticolas refers to the Confederate advance party, a battalion of 180 men from the Second Texas Mounted Rifles, led by Maj. Charles L. Pyron of that regiment. From Fort Craig, Colonel Canby had also sent out an advance party to watch the Texans' movements. This party crossed to the east side of the Rio Grande, confronted Pyron's battalion about 9:00 A.M., and was soon reinforced by Union cavalry, artillery, and infantry under the command of Col. Benjamin S. Roberts, Fifth New Mexico Volunteers. (*O.R.* IV: 138–39, 157–58.)

table land on our left ride rapidly away toward the fort, doubtless to inform Canby that we were reinforcing our troops in the Valley. In high spirits and singing songs, we crossed the valley at the same rapid pace and dismounted among the cotton woods and advanced rapidly (after having hitched our horses) to a slight embankment on our line of defense, which was in the valley. We heard the rapid discharge of small arms on our left, and every half minute, the discharge of heavy artillery warned us that the enemy was throwing their shells and balls at Baylor's men on the left. As soon as we made our appearance they greeted us with a rapid discharge of small arms, but we were none of us hurt, as we laid close to the ground and behind the trees. By looking over the little slant behind which we were lying, we could see the enemy in long lines about 300 yards distant. Not a gun was fired while we were lying there, and we waited anxiously for Teel's artillery to make its appearance, that we might be able to reply to the enemy's artillery, which we feared was playing havoc with our men on the left.

In order to give a more correct idea of the memorable battle of *Val Verde* (green valley) that we fought on this, the 21st of February, the same day of the month that the memorable battle of Manassas was fought, I will draw a sketch of the battle field on the next page and mark it so that our position and our advantages may be understood. Our position was on the right of the high table mountain that lies between this valley and the fort, and our line was a very slight bank of land running across the bottom, but not parallel to the river.[3] In the morning the enemy, both infantry and artillery, were across the river from where our lines approached nearest the river on the left. After we had been lying behind our bank some ten minutes, listening to the balls whistling over our heads and chatting to one another about the extreme probability of there being a *row*, and cautioning one another to keep down heads that no bullet might kill one of our men, five guns of Teel's battery, with Capt. Teel himself, came thundering down and in a moment had taken position directly in front of us and upon the level of the bottom and commenced firing directly at the infantry and artillery across the river, we judged with telling effect.[4] In a moment the enemy had changed

---

3. This was the bank of an old bed of the Rio Grande.

4. About 11:00 A.M., Capt. Trevanion T. Teel, First Texas Artillery, brought a battery of four six-pounder field guns into action at Valverde. In addition, Sibley's men had eleven other cannon. These, however, were all twelve-pounder mountain

their battery and it began to play with its whole force upon Teel's battery, and then we began to feel convinced that we were in a hot place indeed. Shell and round shot and minie bullets came whistling in showers over our heads, bombs burst just behind and before, and trees were shattered and limbs began to fall, a horse or two was shot, and presently they brought back one of Teel's artillery men severely wounded. At almost the same time another was shot dead, but in the hail of bullets Teel stood bravely to his post, and his battery returned the fire of the enemy with great spirit. Presently, the battery across the river ceased playing upon us and opened fire on our left again, and Teel limbered up and moved down to the left. Then we noticed that the enemy had crossed the river with their infantry and were moving rapidly up to the right. After riding 250 yards higher up, we dismounted in a perfect hail of bullets and took our position behind the same bank that had protected us below; but here it was higher.[5] As we were in the act of dismounting, [B. A.] Jones' horse was shot in the thigh, [Sgt. Charles A.] Woodapple's was crippled, and a ball tore a small peel of skin from my right thumb, which bled profusely. Unheeding this, however, I tied my mule to a bending tree and went to the bank. We could see the enemy in strength just before us about 600 yards and advancing rapidly as if to force our lines in. They were taking trees as they approached and [were] firing rapidly upon us. We were lying under the bank, and all but those having *minie* rifles were ordered to reserve their fire for shorter range; but myself and a number of others who have minie guns fired upon them with sufficient rapidity to very well reply to their fire. But about this time their bullets began to play havoc with our horses. Sam Hyatt's was shot and killed instantly. I saw [Louis J.] Berkowitz's fall. Numbers of others about the same time were killed and wounded. One man on my left, in [Capt. David A.] Nunn's Company was shot through the back, as he raised to load, by a flank fire, and fell with heart rending groans. Asking some one to load his gun, which was done, he fired at them again, although he had a wound which proved mortal. About this time, the Ab's had gotten in 300 yards of us, and I began to load and shoot as fast as

---

howitzers of shorter range, and consequently of limited use on the battlefield. (Starr Campaign Letters, p. 172; *O.R.* IX: 513–14.)

5. Peticolas and Co. C fought on the Confederate right throughout the battle. Lieutenant Colonel Scurry commanded the field until noon, when Colonel Green arrived and assumed command. Scurry thereafter led all but four companies of the First Regiment on the far right of the Texan line. (*O.R.* IX: 513–14.)

I could at them.[6] I took good aim every time, though their balls whistled with deadly intent around my head.

Behind this bank four of our boys were wounded. [Cpl.] Al Field was shot in the arm, a flesh wound, as he stood behind a large tree shooting at them, and exclaimed "O God, I'm shot." [William H.] Onderdonk was shot through the mouth and his tongue nearly shot out. He pulled out a part of it which was hanging ragged to the edge of the tongue and cut it off with his knife. He then gave his knife to Al Field and told him to give it to his brother. He was borne off the field. S. Schmidt was shot through both thighs by a minie ball. But they began by this time to pay dearly for getting so close to us. Not a man shot without taking sight, for Texas boys are accustomed to the use of arms and never shoot away their ammunition for nothing. Although our balls were not as numerous as theirs, they went with more deadly intent, and our fire soon became extremely galling. The trees did not effectually protect them. The men shot down right at them, and after the fight had been kept up about half an hour, they retreated precipitately towards the river, and in a few moments two of our small howitzers opened upon their retiring column with killing effect, and they broke lines and ran back out of range. Uncle Jannis [?], of Capt. Nunn's Company, in the fight shot down a man and noticing that though wounded he was still shooting, he said: "Captain, yonder is a d——d son of a —— that I have shot who is lying behind a tree shooting at us. May I go out and kill him?" Capt. Nunn gave the permission, and he went out, but the wounded man begged so hard that he did not kill him, but got four minie guns and ammunition and brought them back to the bank.

James Hughes and [N. B.] Lytle fought with great bravery today. They were the only two men I noticed particularly. Every time I would raise up and shoot and lower my head again to load, Berkowitz would ask me "Did you get one yet?" I could never answer positively in the affirmative, though I thought I made one drop who was out by himself. It was sad to notice, however, how our horses were killed up. When we were ordered to mount to move further up to the right, hardly half of Co. C found horses to mount. Capt. H.[ampton] was afoot. My mule was shot too severely to ride, and it was with the remnant of Co's I and C that the division of the regiment to which we were attached moved to the right. The infantry

---

6. Abolitionists; Federal soldiers. The term may have been unique to Texas Confederates.

of Co's C and I rallied around their captains about the ground where the horses were shot. Wounded and dead horses were hastily stripped, and those that were able to move were turned loose to feed around or to shiver and die till the battle was over. I thought my mule had but a flesh wound, though she shivered and seemed to be suffering intense pain, but the wound proved mortal, as I found after the battle.

After resting a few moments behind the lines and having shells to burst over our heads every time a knot of us got together, we advanced again to the bank and Capt. Nunn took command of us. And now came a sort of lull in the battle. Both parties ceased their firing for a while and paid exclusive attention to maneuvering. We laid under the bank for an hour watching the distant lines of the enemy, and I was surprised and chagrined about this time to notice how very few of our men were on our line. Where were they? Had they left the field entirely, or were the field officers maneuvering them around, that our center was protected for an extent of 250 yards by less than 100 men? I did not know at that time that a heavy force had been left with the wagons as a guard, that they had repulsed Kit Carson and 1000 Mexicans, who had gone round to cut off the train,[7] by a charge, that there were 300 men with the wagons and almost as many more between the battlefield and the train of wagons, too cowardly to risk their lives in the field or, having been there, had quit for frivolous causes. I did not know that we had only about 1500 men of our whole force in the field and that our enemy were 6000 strong, with six pieces of 6 and 12-pound artillery and two 18-pounders upon the field.[8] This I learned afterwards. The enemy crossed the river with their artillery in the evening and brought

---

7. Peticolas is in error here. Colonel Carson, with his regiment, the First New Mexico Volunteers, was approaching the battlefield and was soon fighting on the opposite end of the Union line from Peticolas. These native troops fought well at Valverde, helping smash the Texan assaults on the Federal right flank. (*O.R.* IX: 496, 502–3.)

8. Although exact figures cannot be determined, Sibley probably had about 2,000 men at Valverde. Canby had a total of about 3,800 men at Fort Craig. His field force of approximately 2,500 troops included only about 1,200 regulars, with the balance being volunteers and militiamen without significant experience or adequate training. The Federal force had eight guns: Capt. Robert R. Hall's battery of two twenty-four-pounder howitzers; and Capt. Alexander McRae's battery of one twelve-pounder mountain howitzer, two twelve-pounder field howitzers, and three six-pounder field guns. See also Richard K. McMaster and George Ruhlen, "The Guns of Valverde," *Password* 5 (1960): 26–28.

over their whole force, as well as I could judge. We commenced the fight about 8 o'clock; about 2 they made the attack again on both wings and the center with their artillery, and against 9 pieces we could reply but poorly with our four 6-pounders. Our howitzers did not do a great deal of good, being too short and light. The infantry with their long-range small arms, too, began to throw balls thick and close upon our lines, and now the firing began to be heavy all up and down the line. We would only shoot at intervals with our small arms, as they were of an inferior kind to theirs, and now I began to feel almost disheartened. As long as we laid behind the sand banks our own lives were in comparative safety, but every few moments some one would be wounded or killed, and our horses were being badly shot to pieces.

About this time, 6 pieces of artillery ran out and planted in point-blank range of us and began to play grape and shell upon us.[9] In a moment or two, up came Teel with two guns and planted them within ten yards of where I was lying and opened fire upon the enemy. Every man had been shot from one piece but one. He called for volunteers to help work the guns. Half a dozen men sprang to his assistance, [B. A.] Jones among them. Col. Green, upon his horse, was just in our rear. He was asked what he thought of the fight. He replied that he did not think it was intended to bring on a decisive battle. [Lt. Thomas P.] Ochletree was at his side. [Samuel A.] Lockridge, Major of the 2nd Regiment, Scurry, Col. of the 1st, were on foot in the ranks, keeping the men from lifting their heads to expose them to the leaden shower. And now the battle was indeed hot. Slowly but surely, the heavy columns of infantry and the artillery on the left were driving back our lines, and the close, heavy cannonading on the left showed us that our men could not long hold their lines against the galling fire. The enemy's artillery had nearly reached the position on our left occupied by Teel's battery in the morning. In two minutes a raking fire up our line on the side of the bank would slay the last man of us. The bombs and grape were bursting and flying all around us and around Colonel Green, and sweeping the trees and the bottom far behind us. At this critical moment, Col. Green said: "We must charge that battery, boys." Some ran for their horses; he dashed at them and drove them back to the

---

9. McRae's Battery. For a Union description of this and subsequent artillery actions, see Bell, "The Campaign of New Mexico," pp. 63–65. See also Marion C. Grinstead, *Life and Death of a Frontier Fort: Fort Craig, New Mexico, 1854–1885* (Socorro, N.M.: Socorro County Historical Society, 1973).

Peticolas's sketch of the Battle of Valverde. Battle line of mounted Texans in foreground, with Hall's U.S. battery of twenty-four-pounder howitzers in the center, supported by Union regular infantry and the First New Mexico Volunteer Regiment. View is looking west from the base of Black Mesa toward the Rio Grande, and shows the extreme left flank of the Texan position. Balance of sketch missing. (Peticolas Journal)

bank: "Back, men, back! Would you disgrace yourself and your country here? Remember you are Texians!" Scurry, understanding the motives of their move better, exclaimed [*sic*] the charge must be made on foot. The order was passed rapidly by the aides. Scurry and Lockridge, rising at once, said: "Charge, boys, charge!", and at the command 200 men, a mere handful, started up and with a wild yell dashed forward through the shower of minie balls and grape towards the belching cannon and the solid lines of infantry supporting them. Lockridge, with heart of iron, led us on. Capts. [Charles M.] Lesueur, [William P.] Hardeman, and [James M.] Crosson followed close behind, shouting as they waved their swords: "Come on, my boys, don't stop here." As we neared the lines, our short-range guns began to play with telling effect upon their lines, they wavered, they fled, and we poured in our deadly fire upon them. "This is mine," exclaimed Lockridge, placing his hand on a cannon. At that moment he was shot dead. His last words were: "Go on my boys, don't stop here."[10] The artillery men, brave to the last, were shot down at their posts. Two guns were loaded when we took them. A gunner was just about to touch one off. One of our men who had just killed one of the artillery men, was up on the caisson. He leveled his pistol at the gunner, who in an instant thrust his fuse into the caisson box, which blew up with a dreadful explosion.[11] But we had repulsed them, and they were crowding across the river. We rushed up to the bank and poured a deadly fire upon them. Just about the time our first men reached the cannon, we heard heavy firing on our left and knew that the battle was hot there. The left wing had charged upon horseback and had been repulsed with loss by the heavy lines of infantry, who reserved their fire till our men had gotten

10. This desperate charge was the turning point of the Battle of Valverde. It created panic among the raw native soldiers of the Third and Fifth New Mexico Volunteers, and the panic spread to some of the nearby regular infantrymen. These troops were the principal supports for McRae's Battery. (*O.R.* IX: 490–91.)

11. In this gallant defense of the key to the Union line, Captain McRae, a Southerner loyal to the Union and "deaf to the seductions of family and friends," along with Lt. Lyman Mishler and all of the battery's noncommissioned officers, fell among their guns. The only surviving officer of the battery, Lt. Joseph M. Bell, was thrice wounded. At Lockridge's statement of ownership of the cannon, McRae is supposed to have shouted to his men, "Shoot the son of a bitch." Regarding the caisson explosion, a nearby Colorado Volunteer observed: "When the battery was gone, one of the battery boys sprang on a magazine which was near, cried 'Victory or death' and then coolly fired his pistol into the ammunition. One long, loud crash and all was over for that brave boy." (*O.R.* IX: 492; Bell, "The Campaign of New Mexico," p. 64; Ickis Diary, entry for 21 February 1862.)

in about 120 yards of them. But now they had to change their position and turned a raking fire in upon us, but nothing would stand before our victorious forces. Their own cannon were rapidly drawn down towards the left, where we were driving them back, and fired upon them with telling effect. Teel, too, came on with two pieces and poured a deadly fire in upon their retreating columns fast making for the fort.

I thought that I had experienced a good many moments of exquisite pleasure, but never before have I felt such perfect happiness as I did when we took the battery from our enemy. Then I knew the tide of battle was changed, and my feelings changed with it. We did not pursue any of our foes across the river, for it was about 5 o'clock, and both men and horses were completely worn out, but we raised a loud shout of gladness, and I did not forget to feel thankful to the great *King of Kings*, who is the God of Battles.

Thus, after fighting 9 hours did we win the battle of *Val Verde* on a day which we will all recollect. We camped on the river in strange confusion at night, wagons and men all together and regiments mixed, for a flag of truce had come over as soon as our firing ceased, asking for an armistice of 24 hours to bury the dead, which was granted. A cross on my plan shows the point from which we charged. We lost 40 killed and 140 wounded. Their loss is, as well as we can learn, about 350 killed and 400 wounded. We took a number of prisoners who gave us this as the estimate.[12] Our Wagonmaster was taken prisoner this morning before the trains started, while out hunting the missing mules.

Saturday, 22 February 1862

We buried our dead today; a sad duty. Prisoners were exchanged, and the old Wagonmaster came in this evening, greeted by a loud cheer from our regiment. Mexicans were released on oath not to fight against the Confederacy. We took supper last night on provisions abandoned by the Abs in their flight. Light bread, coffee, sugar, and bacon for three days were all snugly stored away in their hav-

---

12. Peticolas's figures for Confederate losses are fairly accurate. Colonel Green reported 36 killed, 150 wounded, and 1 missing. Subsequently, 43 of the wounded Texans died. His figures on Union casualties are naturally less accurate. Canby reported 68 killed, 160 wounded, and 35 missing. Of those wounded, 17 later died, making Federal and Confederate losses about equal at Valverde, although the percentage loss among Texans was greater. (*O.R.* IX: 493, 521, 647; *San Antonio Herald,* 3 May 1862.)

Graves of Texans killed at the Battle of Valverde and buried on the battlefield. (Arizona Historical Society)

ersacks. [Sgt. William T.] Davis got two horses and 3 overcoats. He gave me a horse and overcoat.

I went over the battle ground today (morning) and looked mournfully at the dead horses and men. Lieut. Col. [John S.] Sutton, of the 3rd Regiment was dangerously wounded. [Maj. Henry W.] Raguet was shot in the leg. Tant [J. K. T.] Walton was killed when the left was repulsed. Capt. [Marinus van der] Huevel, of Co. G, was shot through the left eye, leading on his column. He was a brave soldier, the soul of his company, and had been in 8 pitch[ed] battles in Europe. I saw him lying in state (as it were) upon the battle field. Kit Carson's regiment deserted him after the fight, and numbers of Mexicans fled, not to the fort, but from it, "the living to suffer, the wounded to die," and the whole federal army, the very pick of which we fought, is almost demoralized. This is the tale we hear from deserters and Mexican prisoners.[13]

I feel extremely sad today. My feelings have undergone another change, another wave has come over me; the usual reaction, however, after any very great excitement. Our wounded men are all doing pretty well. I was in about 50 yards of the guns when the caisson exploded, and as soon as I got to the cannon I thought of turning a piece round and blazing away at the enemy on the other bank of the river, but no one would help me. Every one was busy shooting at the foe in and across the river. Two of the pieces were loaded when taken and were shot afterwards at the retreating foe

---

13. Actually, these were Col. Miguel E. Pino's men from the Second New Mexico Volunteers.

across the river. The mortality amongst them in the river was terrible. The shot guns then came into play and did great execution.[14] I took several shots at separate men across the river, but killed none, as I suppose I shot too high. In making the charge, at every discharge of the cannon, the men would fall, and prisoners informed us that they thought they were playing terrible havoc with us. Some 30 or 40 prisoners were taken, two captains amongst them. Of the artillery company (enemy), every man was killed or wounded save 6 privates and a sergeant. Two other companies were cut entirely to pieces, and some of them were Pike's Peak men. J. O. Wheeler escorted one of the prisoner captains to camp. Ben White behaved with great bravery. But [Cpl. Albert] Glock and 4 others deserted the field, went to the wagons, and could not be persuaded to go out and repulse the enemy's cavalry on the hill when they tried to cut off the trains. Liquor and sweet spirits of nitre was found in considerable quantities on the field, no doubt to make the soldiers brave by the use of it. [Lt. Col. Benjamin S.] Roberts commanded in the morning and Canby in the evening. The governor of the territory was there to see us gloriously whipped, and doubtless his mortification was intense to see that it was not done.[15] The most laughable sight on the whole field was to see Capt. H[ampton], when our horses were being killed up so badly, crawling up to the sand bank on his hands and knees. After the attack in the morning, and the repulse, I saw no more of the captain but once, till late in the evening. Then he had the infantry, of which he was one, rallied about 150 yards in the rear of the sand bank, behind the sand banks. He did not take position, however, on our line to help defend it, and I left him.

We got about 130 stand of small arms, 6 pieces of artillery, and a considerable quantity of ammunition, several six-shooters, and a considerable number of cast-off overcoats. [J. T.] Williams found a silver watch and overcoat, and I picked up a blanket in place of the one I had thrown off. In the lull of the battle, I went to where I had stripped my mule and got my blanket, which I left wrapped around me till the charge was made. It snowed a little about the time the attack of the enemy was fiercest on our lines in the morning, and I began to feel uneasy lest my caps should not fire well, and it was

---

14. No more than a dozen Federal soldiers were killed in crossing the Rio Grande, and probably that many more were wounded. (*O.R.* IX: 493.)

15. Peticolas is correct on this score. For Gov. Henry Connelly's report on the Battle of Valverde, see *O.R.* IX: 637–39.

gloomy and cold all the evening. The whole talk in camp today was about the fight, of course, and every man was recounting his individual exploits with great zest, not recollecting the old saying: "a fool blows his own horn, a smart man gets his blown for him, and a man of genius would die rather than blow his own horn or get any other man to do it for him."

Sunday, 23 February 1862

About 12 o'clock we took up the line of march again up the country,[16] left the wagons for want of teams, burnt a number of saddles and old clothes, and traveled about 6 miles and crossed the river, which took us all day. 200 mounted men went up from Craig last night and the governor with them. 8 companies of our men and two pieces of artillery were sent up the country. We passed through a small Mexican village and camped late at night in the broad valley, where wood was very hard to get. We got some 3000 $ worth of goods out of a store belonging to a captain who was in the fight.[17] These things were confiscated; also some work oxen and a large flock of sheep. The wearing apparel was divided out to the different regiments and companies, and we had a dinner and breakfast of mutton.

Monday, 24 February 1862

We laid in camp today, and the quartermasters were busy dividing out the plunder that had been confiscated. Found it very difficult to get wood this morning; had to pull down dead limbs from high up in the cottonwood trees with a rope, which was not a very expeditious way of getting it, for it requires a considerable amount of skill to throw a rope over a high limb. The battle is a topic of conversation not yet exhausted, and the number of yankees

---

16. On the day after the battle, Sibley sent two officers to demand the surrender of Fort Craig. Canby's refusal left the Texan commander with a serious dilemma. Although he had won a tactical victory at Valverde, his men had only about five days' rations left. With a strong enemy garrison and post in his rear, he had the choice of fighting his way back to the Mesilla Valley or continuing north with the hope of capturing Federal supplies at Polvadera, Albuquerque, Santa Fe, and finally, Fort Union. He chose the latter course, but traveled very slowly northward along the Rio Grande, giving Union troops adequate time to destroy or move their supplies.

17. This camp was near the site of abandoned Fort Conrad, just upriver from Col. Robert H. Stapleton's store and the village of Valverde. (Howell Journal, entry for 23 February 1862.)

murdered in these accounts of individual exploits is astonishing. The day is quite warm, and everything betokens coming spring.

Tuesday, 25 February 1862

We marched today about 10 miles and camped about 3 o'clock in the evening in a wide valley. Wood is extremely scarce here, too, and the grass is not worth a straw for horses. Several of the sick men carried today on litters. Lieut. Col. Sutton died in camp on Monday, and today when we got to camp, it was found that Lieut. [David R.] McCormick, of Co. F, was very low. He died tonight.

Wednesday, 26 February 1862

We buried McCormick this morning, and today more wounded men were packed in litters than there were yesterday. We passed through several ranches and an old town called San Antonio today. I neglected to state that last night an express came down from above stating that the Companies above had taken 200 prisoners and 300 stand of arms and some 150 mules, and nearly the same number of horses; also 8000 barrels of flour and a number of Government wagons. The Mexican pickets fired on our men, but hurt no one, and as soon as they had thrown 1 cannon ball into the town, a white flag announced that they had surrendered. This was at Socorro.[18] To this place we were to go today 14 miles, but it was late in the evening before we reached camp. Socorro is a place of considerable size and has 2 little villages on the north side of it, about 2 miles off, between which we are camped tonight; one is on the right and the other on the left bank of the river.[19] We got wood by kicking up little stumps that were rotten at the bottom and projected an inch or two above the ground. Coming on today with the wagons, as most of the mounted men of our company did, for the Captain was with the infantry behind. I fell in with one of [Willis L.] Lang's men, Captain of the Lancers in the 2nd Regiment, who informed me that the charge in which they lost so many men in the battle was on the extreme right, and that but one company charged, as he affirms that Col. Green countermanded the order before it was executed, but

---

18. These were New Mexico militiamen, commanded by Col. Nicolás Pino. They had been sent away from Fort Craig after the Battle of Valverde. With few exceptions, including Colonel Pino, they had little further interest in defending the territory. (*O.R.* IX: 605.)

19. These were the villages of Escondido and Parida.

"Hospital C. S. A. & Church, Socoro, N. M." Present-day San Miguel
Church in Socorro, sketched by a convalescent Texas soldier and copied
later by Peticolas. (Arizona Historical Society)

that Capt. Lang did not hear the counter command. He says that
only a few broke through the lines of the enemy, that a good many
turned back on seeing they were not supported by the other three
companies that were with them. This charge, according to him (and
he was in it), was made in the morning and must have been extremely high up on the right, for I saw nothing of it, though I watched
the battle, as far as I could see it, very closely.[20]

The wounded [of our regiment] were all left at Socorro this
evening, and all the rest are to go there tomorrow, where they will
remain until cured of their wounds. A few remain to care for the
sick, as they are not able to stand the fatigues of travel; so say the
doctors. Al Field is one that is to be left, as he is not well enough to
walk. The question of dismounting several companies of the First
regiment is seriously debated on account of the number of horses
killed, and as there is no forage for horses in this part of the country,
either corn, hay, or grass, and it grows scarcer as we approach Santa
Fe, and the men see a prospect of their animals starving. The idea

---

20. This charge by the only remaining lancer unit, Co. B, Second Regiment, was
bloodily repulsed by Dodd's Independent Company of Colorado Volunteers and by
regulars of Capt. P. W. L. Plympton's battalion. (Bell, "The Campaign of New Mexico,"
p. 62; Ickis Diary, entry for 21 February 1862.)

is not as repugnant to them as one would naturally suppose it would be to the cowboy of Texas.

Thursday, 27 February 1862

We laid in camps today making preparations to turn over our horses to the government at their appraised values. I had my horse that Davis gave me appraised before turning him over; he was appraised, with the saddle, at $110.[21] The whole regiment turns over horses today and from here forward will be infantry, I suppose, as I don't expect we will ever take horses enough to mount the regiment again. Our provisions have grown short, too; we have been a day without bread, and there is no more bread stuff in the train. Scurry says that if we don't take government stores to supply us at Albikirque that we will have to press stores into service. We hear nothing more of the enemy at Craig. Aid-de-camp Ochletree, who stayed at the fort Sunday, informed us on his return that Canby was doing nothing that day. He incidentally mentioned toasts that he drank at the Colonel's table, "To the southern Confederacy and our great victory," etc., in the same style. Since that time, we have heard various reports of their intentions. Some of them are that they are preparing a new battery and intend to take the field again; others that they are crossing over the mountains to Ft. Union, there to make a stand again. We don't know what they are doing. Another report says that 3000 yankee volunteers from in and around Pike's Peak are ahead of us. We fought one company from Pike's Peak in the battle of *Val Verde*, and they were dreadfully cut to pieces.

Our horses are all turned over, and afoot and without bread, the regiment is more depressed than it has been for months, but they are willing to live on beef, poor as it is, to accomplish our object. Several Captains who had been speaking of resigning after Ft. Craig was taken, resigned this morning and are going home: one (Capt. Nunn) of the 1st and three from the 2nd Regiment. These captains did not get along very well with their men and had been petitioned to resign. Al Field took leave of us this evening, and Morris Lichtenstein, who goes back to nurse the sick. [Philip] Meyer also went back for the same purpose.

---

21. Peticolas was never paid by Confederate authorities for this horse and equipment, which were his personal property, nor were any of the other men of the First Regiment, although they continued to request compensation for two years after the New Mexico campaign. (Noel, *A Campaign from Santa Fe to the Mississippi*, p. 31.)

Friday, 28 February 1862

We took our first march as infantry today, about 10 miles, and many a foot was blistered, but upon the whole we made the trip very well considering that we had no bread for breakfast. There was one four-bits in the mess, which was spent today for bread, and tonight we had a supper which we relished exceedingly.[22] We also drew a pound of meal to the man tonight, which will afford us one meal with bread for 3 days. We never eat but two meals. I have a blister on my heel about as large as a quarter of a dollar tonight, from which the skin is peeled, but I washed my feet thoroughly in cold water, and they feel tolerably comfortable now.

Saturday, 1 March 1862

We are now beginning to experience about the greatest of the manifold hardships of war. Upon the battlefield there was the fierce din of conflict and the danger to face, but we had our courage and our convictions of the importance of winning the day to sustain us. When we stood at the graves with arms reversed and saw our comrades in arms buried, [we] were naturally low-spirited and sorrowful, but we knew that they died nobly with their "backs to the field and their feet to the foe" and that for them no shrill bugle blast would sound to rouse to arms and battle again till the resurrection morn when Gabriel has undertaken to bugle exclusively for the occasion. But to trudge along day after day with nothing to eat save beans, with no teams fit to transport our baggage, and no forage, and then to see our officers, every one of them with great sacks of flour and sides of bacon, living high while the men are really suffering for something to eat—to go from early breakfast till late supper, and feel the weakness and gnawing of hunger—hunger for the staff of life—is a feature of soldiering without any redeeming trait.

We traveled 10 or 12 miles today through very heavy sand, and as our regiment was on guard today behind the wagons, we did not get to camp till in the night. I left the company when the train of wagons first stalled, and came on ahead. Found wood scarcer than it has yet been, and Buffalo Chips the only fuel. It was bitter cold today, and the wind blew the sand in clouds across our way and in our faces. Cooking tonight was a more desperate undertaking than

---

22. As a sergeant, Peticolas was responsible for drawing rations for himself and seven other men. This "mess" then did their own cooking and augmented their fare by whatever means seemed appropriate. Their camp this evening was at or near Polvadera.

it has yet been. I was tempted to give it up two or three times. We are camped in a very strong position tonight; a semicircular bank closes in the camp towards the river, and the whole valley is on a level with the top of the bank, save the little hollow where we are camped.[23] The battery is on the level of the valley, while the whole camp is protected from any fire on this side of the river by the aforesaid bank. I knew directly I saw the camp that the field officers had gotten some news either from above or below, and sure enough, when I got into camp I heard that the enemy at Albikirque were rallying the citizens and intended to make a stand against us there. However, in our present situation the enemy is the last thing we dread, and some were rather glad to hear of it, for they thought it was proof that the Federals have something there to defend.

Sunday, 2 March 1862

We laid in camp till noon today and then traveled 5 or 6 miles and camped near a little town, the name of which I did not learn.[24] We were furnished wood from town, and our camp was just below a ditch on the hillside from which the town and valley is irrigated. We passed several ranches on the way. This part of New Mexico is more desirable than any I have yet seen. The valley is very wide and fertile and is thickly settled. Some of the churches are very neatly built, and the houses, inside, are very well furnished. Some of them are papered and some of them neatly whitewashed, and they are perfectly air-tight.

Monday, 3 March 1862

Traveled 10 or 12 miles today and camped again on the confines of a little Mexican settlement,[25] from which we got wood again, though we did not get it without some trouble, for Scurry informed us that we need [not] put ourselves to any trouble to get it, as we would have it handed to us; but none was hauled, and the end of it was that Scurry bought of some of the inhabitants the roof poles off a fodder shed and issued two poles to the company; not enough to make a cup of coffee for us. We managed, however, to press enough into service to get a supper and breakfast of beans.

---

23. Across the Rio Grande from the village of La Jolla. (Howell Journal, entry for 1 March 1862.)

24. Sabinal. (Smith Journal, p. 136; Giesecke Diary, entry for 2 March 1862.)

25. The camp was near the town of Belen.

Tuesday, 4 March 1862

The first Regiment parted from the brigade this morning, passing through more Mexican settlements, and crossed the river to go up on the right hand side. It was laughable as well as disagreeable to see the regiment, barelegged and barefooted, wading the ice-cold water of the river and to hear their exclamations as they waded into deep water. Some of the captains (Lesueur, Hardeman, Crosson, [William L.] Alexander, and the German Captain [Julius Giesecke]) waded; the others crossed on horseback, being *too delicate* to wade. Hardeman said that whenever he could not lead his men where they were to go, that he would take them back home. Two men who were crossing on horseback got a proper dunking. The horses stumbled and fell down in the deepest part of the river, and the men got thoroughly wet. We traveled in all about ten miles today and camped in a cottonwood grove where we were not so much troubled about wood as we have been.[26] About 12 o'clock I got very hungry and dropped out of ranks to see if I could not make a raise of something to eat at some of the numerous Mexican houses that were scattered all along the way. I asked in Spanish at the first place where I saw any of the inhabitants, for a little bread. They said they had none, but one of the women sitting out there in the sun held a conversation with one of the men for a few moments, tears came to her eyes as she spoke, and she ended [up] giving him a key, and he told me to come with him. This was close to the road. As soon as I started off, [Frank D.] Kneiber, who knew that my knowledge of Spanish was very limited, left ranks and came on too, and after a while I saw [B. A.] Jones trudging very slowly after us. We all got to the house together, and while a boy was cooking us something to eat, the man of the house was recounting his trials with the Federals when they tried to force him into the service. They knocked him down, and he showed us a bayonet wound where they stabbed him trying to force him along any how. He told us that there was many a man sick that they had forced into the service, but that no one was allowed to stop or rest on that account, but was forced along by the federals. He gave us broiled beef, a sort of mush with sugar and grease in it, and eggs, for dinner and seemed to give with a free will. I gave him my tobacco and Kneiber did the same. We told him we had no money, but he said he wanted no pay and could hardly be persuaded to take Frank's tobacco.

---

26. Near Peralta, the scene of future fighting, some twenty miles south of Albuquerque.

Last night, Judge [Spruce M.] Baird, from Nacogdoches, Texas, formerly governor of New Mexico,[27] came down from his residence near Albikirque and informed us that the Federals had been unable to make a stand at Albikirque and had burned everything they had there. He said that they burnt hay enough to last the whole Brigade 6 months, and destroyed everything. He traveled with us today and talked a good deal with the boys, speaking encouragingly of our prospects for provisions at Albikirque. He says that the inhabitants of the towns above are all for us and are willing to sell to us anything they have on the credit of our government. He says that in Alberkeurque it would take a very strong force to get us out, and that in Santa Fe, 40,000 men would hardly do it. We got flour tonight, and bread tasted very sweet to us after living on poor beef and beans for so many days.

Wednesday, 5 March 1862

My feet were very sore this morning from my yesterday's walk, and I started early this morning on our journey, intending to take my time and make the 12 miles we have to go with as much ease to myself as possible. Our Journey today is to Judge Baird's residence, and there are two roads, one of them 2 or 3 miles further than the other, but a much better road for wagons, running around through the hills. The other runs up the river bottom and is very sandy indeed. The latter road I took, as I wanted to make my walk as short as possible. Passed through a good many Mexican settlements; in fact one is hardly out of sight of Mexican houses anywhere while travelling up this part of the valley. I suffered more with my feet today than I have yet done, although I walked very slowly. I got to camp between sundown and dark, and as wood was very scarce, I went to picking up dry cow chips. We camped in a quarter of a mile of Judge Baird's residence, from which the confederate flag was waving as we came into sight. We got wood, too, from his house.[28] He made the regiment a present of enough to cook supper and break-

---

27. Baird had come to New Mexico in 1848, when Texas claimed that part of the territory east of the Rio Grande. Appointed judge of Santa Fe County, Texas, he lost the position when that state ceded its claim to New Mexico in the Compromise of 1850. Baird chose to remain and practice law, however, and was appointed attorney general of the territory in 1860. He was an ardent Southern sympathizer. (Walter P. Webb and H. Bailey Carroll, eds., *The Handbook of Texas*, 1 [Austin: Texas State Historical Association, 1952], p. 97.)

28. The Baird residence still stands, much modified and in very poor condition, on Shirk Road, in Albuquerque's South Valley.

"Judge Beard's residence, NM. Mch. 6th '62." Peticolas's sketch of the ranch of Judge Spruce M. Baird, located on present-day Shirk Road, in Albuquerque's South Valley. The view is looking eastward from the Rio Grande toward the Manzano Mountains. (Peticolas Journal)

fast with, for which I hope we were all duly thankful. He told us, too, that the Craig forces were the worst whipped set of men he ever saw, that they could not have been, from the most reasonable accounts he heard from the fight, less than 400 men killed dead and about the same number wounded. Most of our men shot too high, and whenever a ball would strike, the wound was generally in a fatal place. Rumor has it now that Canby has left Craig and is making for Ft. Union to make another stand; that he has only 800 men with him; that all the Mexicans have left him, glad of an excuse to leave. Baird says that to his certain knowledge there were 8000 men at Craig and 1300 were regulars and Pikes Peak men. Of these, the morning after the fight, only 900 were there to answer to their names at roll call.[29] [The day before yesterday,] 2 companies of regulars were in the settlements through which we passed today, and we kept a look out for them all day today. The Command went the long road through the hills, and when they got to camp about ½ past 8 o'clock, every man was mad enough to bite a tenpenny nail in two. Every one swore they had walked 23 miles; that the officers were fools for marching them so far around instead of taking them the short road, etc., etc. I don't know when I have seen the regiment so universally mad. In fact, for such green Volunteers, scarce 3 months from all the comforts of a home life in an enlightened country, we have had pretty rough experiences. I never thought I would ever be so pressed by hunger as to ask for bread when I had no means of paying for it, but I have done it, and without shame too.

Thursday, 6 March 1862

We are lying in camp today and the Brigade officers are feasting and making merry at Judge Baird's. The current *on dits* are that the Governor has ordered the federals to leave the territory and is prepared to turn it over to the S.C. [Southern Confederacy]; that 6000 Mexicans under a certain nameless Mexican Col. have attacked and taken Ft Union, where Baird says there were only 4 Co's of Regulars, and that now the Confederate [flag] is flying over the place; that Pyron at Albikirque has captured 25 wagon loads of flour and 4 Federal prisoners, having six of his men taken (he went on ahead of

---

29. All these rumors were false or exaggerated. Canby was still at Fort Craig with his regulars, Colorado Volunteers, and Kit Carson's New Mexico Volunteers. (*O.R.* IX: 649.)

Although Peticolas did not enter Albuquerque until later, other Texans occupied the town on 2 March 1862. Peticolas sketched the "House in Alberkirque" during April 1862. (Arizona Historical Society)

us);[30] that 16,000 bls. of flour were taken on the other side of the river. Gov. [*sic*] Canby's store has been confiscated. The sayings about the flour are doubtless true. The others I give for what they are worth. We are drawing flour enough to feed us men and are living better than we have for some time before.

Friday, 7 March 1862

We are lying in camp today while stores of every kind, from sutler's stores around, are being collected together for our use; and now, while lying in camp just two weeks from the day of our battle of *Val Verde*, I will recount some of the incidents of the battle which will prove interesting should I ever get home.

When we first reached the field and were lying under the shelf of land which just concealed us from the enemy by lying flat on the ground, the boys chatted as unconcernedly as I ever heard them in my life, though shell and minie bullets were whistling thick and fast all the time. James [Hughes] came near going fast asleep while we were lying there. After Teel got down with his battery and they began to play round shot and shell upon him, one 6-pound ball struck some distance out on the prairie and rolled nearly to the place where we were lying. [W. H.] Onderdonk crawled out to it in spite of our expostulations and got it. After we had looked at it, Onderdonk insisted that we should give it to Teel to shoot back at them, as it might kill some of them. About this time I noticed one of Teel's sergeants of artillery squatting behind the trees and looking very much scared every time the shell would come booming over, and making a good many exclamations suggestive of alarm. One of the lieutenants came up about this time and sternly ordered him to his post at the gun. When we moved our position higher up on the right, just before I dismounted, a ball peeled my right thumb just below the root of the nail, but I did not feel it, though it bled profusely.

---

30. Major Pyron's battalion of Baylor's regiment was acting as the vanguard of Sibley's army of New Mexico. They entered Albuquerque on 2 March, after Union forces had removed or destroyed almost all the military supplies and rations stored in the town. Five days later, several companies of the Second Regiment occupied Albuquerque, raising a Confederate flag on the plaza, firing a thirteen-gun salute, and camping in the town. There Sibley joined them and sent Pyron's battalion on to Santa Fe, which had been evacuated by Federal troops and the territorial government on 4 March. Despite destruction of the military supplies, Sibley's troops captured or confiscated enough material in and around Albuquerque to last them for approximately forty days. (Smith Journal, p. 137; Howell Journal, entry for 7 March 1862; Giesecke Diary, entry for 7 March 1862.)

Williams said that he was tickled wonderfully at one man at the sand bank who was making desperate efforts to shoot his gun without having cocked it. When Onderdonk was shot, some one who was near said, "Look at poor Donk." [Cpl. Lovell J.] Bartlett, who was standing behind a tree shooting, looked and was so much taken aback that he shot off his gun without having taken the rammer out of the barrel. It was a musketoon and had the rammer attached to the gun. It was shot off, however, and fell against the sand bank, but unfit for further use. Bart got another gun.

When the fire was hottest and our horses were being killed so, one man of Co. K lying near me was shot and rolled over, uttering heartrending groans. This for a moment unnerved me and I thought, "that man makes a great fuss for a small hurt." I thought he was only grazed down the back as he lay, but was mistaken. He died from the wound. He got some one, however, to load his gun and shot again before he gave it up.

During the lull in the fight the suspense began to be very painful. I began to be weary (1 P.M.) and heartily wished the battle was over. I ate a little piece of dried beef and suffered for water. About this time I also changed my cartridges from the bottom of my box to the top, having shot away almost every one of those on top in the morning fight. When the Pikes Peak men who had been crowding us so in the morning, and taking advantage of the timber, began to retreat when our fire got too hot for them, we rained the bullets at them and Williams says that Lieut. [Ludwig von] Roeder (who had been lying close in the sand all the morning), after we had all pretty much stopped firing on them because they were too far, jumped up and fired two barrels of his six-shooter at them at 1500 yards distance. Roeder's long-range pistol has become a topic of conversation since.

I saw several horses horribly wounded. A cannon ball shot off the right forefoot of one in 10 yards of me. Another had both forelegs shot off, and the last I saw of him he was trying to use and stand on the shattered stumps. When the order was given in the evening to charge, I was directly in front of the enemy's artillery, which was throwing grape shot with fearful rapidity. I hated to get up from behind the sand bank very much indeed, and after I had gotten up and gotten some 10 yards from the bank on the way to the cannons, I saw that a great many had not started from the sand bank and I paused a moment to entreat them to come on. "Charge, boys, charge! It is the only thing that can save us," I recollect saying, and a few more having started, I rushed on towards the battery, for I knew I could be in no greater danger than I then was. Though a good many of our Company saw me and went near to me, I saw no one I knew as I ran, for my eyes were fixed on the cannon. In the charge a minie ball shot through Abe [Ebenezer] Hanna's hat, grazed his head, and knocked him flat. He was not hurt, however, and got up and came on again. Grape shot plowed up the dust before me and whistled around me and past me as I ran, but no one struck me. I chose the openest ground right in front of the enemy's battery to run on, where there were fewest men, for I knew that the cannoneers of the battery would aim at the thickest bunches of men which were on the right and left of me amongst the trees, and I didn't much fear the minie balls. At least 500 men came up to the right and rushed across the river. All these claimed to have been in the charge, though as far as assisting in taking the battery was concerned, they might as well have been in Guinea. When the left was repulsed, some companies went clear back to the wagons before they could be rallied. Williams was not in the charge but came on past the cannons very shortly after they were taken, and when he got to the river side, he found two wounded men who were lying there groaning. The battle being pretty well over, with the assistance of one or two others of our men, he got a fire built and took the two wounded men to the fire, stripped them of their shoes, put overcoats from dead men over them, and made them as comfortable as the nature of the case would admit. They dragged one of the Ab's out of the river, all muddy and nearly frozen, and put him near the fire, too, and then another wounded man, shot through the jaw and with his face all swollen and the blood dropping from his mouth, crawled up to the fire too. One of the wounded men said, "You have saved my life this time; perhaps sometime I may have the chance to do as much for you." Notwithstanding his good intentions, however, I would decidedly prefer that no one of my mess should ever be in a condition to profit by his good intentions.

After the battle it was amusing to notice with what joy acquaintances shook hands and congratulated each other on being alive. They laughed and danced and shook hands with more real joy than friends must after years of absence in ordinary circumstances. I missed Jas. Hughes and the thought struck me, "He must have been wounded in that charge." Wasting not a moment, I started off to hunt him, and when I met him I shook hands with him with the greatest *vim*. Williams and another man halted a whole column of men with one of the captured pieces as they came rapidly down towards where they were tending the wounded. They proved to be our men. Just before we charged, and while Teel's two 6-pounders were playing upon their battery, Green was sitting on his horse $\frac{1}{2}$ a dozen yards in our rear, shouting, "Take good aim, boys, take good aim! Fire!" to the artillerymen. Scurry, as we hurried down to the left after taking the battery, seemed deeply impressed with the daring of the charge that we had just made. "Well, I never did see such a charge as that," he kept repeating; "I never did see the like." While hurrying to the left in the evening, a riderless horse was going my way. I jumped on him and hurried off looking for Scurry, who I knew was afoot, to give him the horse. I enquired of Col. Green for him; he asked me what I wanted. I told him I wanted to give him [Scurry] my horse, as he was afoot. He said that his horse was shot and could not get about, and proposed that I should give up the horse to him and take his and take care of him for him. I did so, and in a few moments met Col. Scurry, mounted. After the battle was over, as I had seen nothing of Jas. Hughes for some time, not being able to find him, I wandered around over the battle-ground. Fires had been built in various parts of the grounds, and the wounded had been taken to them and laid around with blankets over them, as comfortable as circumstances would permit. It was a sad sight to see these young men, so lately in all the strength and vigor of manhood, now lying pale and weak around these fires, suffering.

Saturday, 8 March 1862

We took up the line of march today in a furious west wind and marched a little north of east out into the mountains, where I understand we will lay by to let the mules recruit a little, as the grass is better there than on the prairie bottoms of the river, and there is wood. Soon after we passed Judge Baird's house, the wind increased to almost a hurricane. Clouds of sand came driving against our backs, and the whole atmosphere was dark with the heavy clouds of sand. The pebbles dashed stingingly against our backs, and our eyes were almost put out by the sand. I put my hat up over my face and thus protected my eyes as much as I could. Fortunately for us, the wind was on our backs and served to help us along, while the damage to our eyes was not so great as it must have been going in the opposite direction. I thought of the Simoons which cross the great deserts of Africa, which could scarcely exceed in violence the wind we experienced. We traveled rapidly and towards evening reached the mountains and passing down a long descent and reached a deep canyon where the wind did not blow with so much violence. We camped about a mile from where we first entered the canyon on a little stream that finds its source at Soda Spring.[31] Wood, though not abundant, is to be had here in reasonable quantities. The high barren rocky mountains are studded with a stunted growth of cedar, which, though green, makes a tolerable fire. Tonight is bitter cold and disagreeable.

Sunday, 9 March 1862

Laid in camp today and the weather, cold, windy, with frequent showers of snow, claims our exclusive attention, for we shiver round the best fire we can make, all wrapped in our overcoats. On guard tonight to crown the sum of my discomforts. We are living now on bread and beef, everything else having given out. Poor meat, for the beef is miserably lean and tough, neither fit to eat broiled or boiled.

Monday, 10 March 1862

Still lying in camp today, but the weather is more pleasant. I read through a novel this evening entitled, "The King and the Cobbler," a small book, but interesting enough to while away an hour with. News reached us last night that our forces met with a severe and decided repulse in Kentucky.[32] The news came through a St. Louis paper. News also that the Ab's have abandoned Santa Fe, which is ours without the firing of a gun. The inhabitants rose *en masse* when the Federals wished to destroy Government stores and property, and told them that they were free to leave, but could not destroy the stores, as they would hold them for us. Capt. [John G.] Phillips has been sent up to take possession for us.[33]

---

31. The First Regiment, along with several companies of the Second and Third regiments, was sent into the Sandia Mountains, east of Albuquerque. They camped in Tijeras, or Carnuel, Canyon, through which ran the most direct road to Fort Union, via the villages of San Antonio, Galisteo, and Glorieta. The water supply here was reliable, if not abundant, while piñon and juniper wood was readily available. This location might have seemed to be a good place to recruit men and animals; however, the weather there during March is often very severe.

32. The repulse to which Peticolas refers was probably the Battle of Mill Springs, fought on 19 January, and one of the earliest Union victories.

33. Captain Phillips commanded the "company of Santa Fe gamblers," or Brigands, recruited by Sibley from the dregs of the capital's society. Some Santa Fe residents may have been pleased to see territorial officials and the Federal garrison

67

Tuesday, 11 March 1862

Moved camp today 5 miles further on towards Santa Fe where there is more wood. The road winds along up through the bottom of the mountains and is splendidly graded, altogether the best road I have traveled for many a day. The mountains on either side are covered with a dense growth of pine and cedar which gradually grows taller and more like timber as the road penetrates deeper and deeper into the mountains. We passed through a sort of ranch when we were in ¹/₂ mile of camp and made a short halt there to wait for the wagons. As I expected, the men had soon visited every hole and corner of the village. There is a mill in the place too, and this attracted the attention of the men in a great degree, as the water power is a stream hardly larger than my arm. We camped on a pleasant south hillside studded with pines and drew the rest of our rations today.[34]

Wednesday, 12 March 1862

Laid in camp today. Quite pleasant weather. Did some washing today. Weather cloudy and still this evening, with strong indications of falling weather.

Thursday, 13 March 1862

Woke this morning with beds covered over an inch deep in snow. Snow still falling. It was amusing to see the men as they woke and looked around with bewildered expressions, raking the snow out of their hats and shoes, but it was not very pleasant. After breakfast I

---

of the city's Fort Marcy leave for Las Vegas, New Mexico, and nearby Fort Union. However, a more typical reaction was that expressed by Mother Magdalen Hayden, mother superior of the Loretto Academy:

> Our poor and distant territory has not been spared. The Texans, without any provocation, have sacked and almost ruined the richest portions and have forced the most respectable families to flee from their homes, not precisely by bad treatment, but by obliging them to deliver to them huge sums of money. To avoid handing over their money to these Texans, the heads of families and some others fled. . . . You can imagine better than I can describe what I felt on seeing all our troops, and that banner under whose shadow I had been raised, leave. . . . The terror which I felt is inexpressible. (Mother Magdalen Hayden to "Sister," 7 May 1862, in Mary J. Straw, *Loretto: The Sisters and Their Santa Fe Chapel* [Santa Fe: Loretto Chapel, 1983], pp. 35–36.)

34. This camp was in and around the village of Tijeras, at the eastern entrance to Tijeras Canyon.

got a novel, "The Monk Knight of St. John," and read it about through. I got in one of the large wagons belonging to [wagonmaster] Burgess' train, and with my feet plunged into a mass of blankets and my overcoat on, I spent the time very comfortably. About noon it stopped snowing and we received orders that camps would be moved this evening to San Antonio, a little town a mile and a half above here.[35] Moved camp this evening and tonight we are quartered on the inhabitants. Four messes, mine included, are quartered in a little old house on the north edge of town, occupied by an old widow woman who is now living in one of the rooms while we use the other two. We build our mess fires outside the house and sleep inside.

Friday, 14 March 1862

I suffered considerably with heartburn last night and had to get up about midnight and get the soda bottle and eat a little. When I rose, I found the ground covered with snow, and for want of water in which to dissolve my soda, I took some snow and ate it, dipping it in the soda as boys would dip bread into a plate of molasses. The snow had fallen during the night and covered everything. It was still falling, and cold as it was, I stood before the opening of the miserable little hacienda in which we are quartered and watched the flakes and the green pines by the misty moonlight. Morning dawned cold and dreary. The men arose from their hard but comfortable couches and began to make preparations for getting breakfast as best they could. News from below came to me today: 17 of our wounded at Socoro are dead. Capt. Lang, 2nd Regt, who was severely wounded, killed himself. The rest are doing well. I traded my Bowie today for a tremendous weapon, about 2 feet long and made of first-rate metal. It is a bowie knife, but more formidable in the hands of a man able to wield it than a sword.

Saturday, 15 March 1862

Weather quite pleasant today save that it is windy and this evening growing very cold. Card playing is the principal amusement. On guard again tonight in the place of Sam[uel R.] Hyatt, Corporal, who is very unwell. On picket 1/2 a mile down the road the way we

---

35. There are several San Antonios in New Mexico. The immediate area around this village is also known as Cedar Crest. The road to Fort Union passed northward from Tijeras, through San Antonio and along the eastern base of the Sandia Mountains, following closely the present alignment of New Mexico Highway 14.

came. We stop at a Mexican's house and he gives us leave to sleep inside in a room larger than any I have yet entered in San Antonio. He treats us finely. His lady spread a bed for me tonight, and there is a warm fire in the hearth and a candle burning in the room, by the light of which I am writing. It is altogether the most comfortable quarters I have yet found to stand guard in. The room is lofty and neatly whitewashed. Just now the men are all lying around on the floor, some asleep and some talking in a low tone. But the coughing is distressing. I tried to make the owner of the ranch sensible how much we were all obliged to him, and they kindly furnished us with pillows and made us comfortable, telling us we were welcome. I am now writing upon one of the long high settees, so common in Mexican houses, that sit along the wall. They are made with a long-legged bench with a long bolster of wool or blankets perhaps and then covered with a gaily striped Mexican blanket which hangs down to the floor and conceals the feet and legs of the benches. I think I will retire to enjoy for the first time since Aug. 22nd, 1861, the luxury of sleeping on a bed!!

Sunday, 16 March 1862

The Lord's Day once more. Alas! Sometimes I almost forget the day entirely, so much does it resemble other days in camp life. May a Good God soon deliver us from this unnatural war that has been forced upon us.

This morning about 1/2 an hour after breakfast there was a demand made by Major Raguet for 20 volunteers to go 1 1/2 miles to capture a train of wagons on a road to the right of this place, supposed to be a yankee train.[36] Escort reported to be 20. In 3 minutes 25 or 30 of our men were ready with guns and ammunition and we started at quick time across the piny hills. We reached the road in a marvelously short space of time, and finding that the wagons we were after had passed on, we hastened on at a long stride, and all the horseback officers struck a lope. We walked nearly or quite 3 miles at a double quick and were beginning to think that we would not catch them at all, when we turned a point of wood and caught sight of them. They were camped, and turned out to be a party of Mexicans traveling with a passport from Gen'l Sibley. After coughing for 5 minutes, we all started back again, and I took a sketch of

---

36. This road, which paralleled the main road traveled by the Texans, is known today as Rider's Ranch Road.

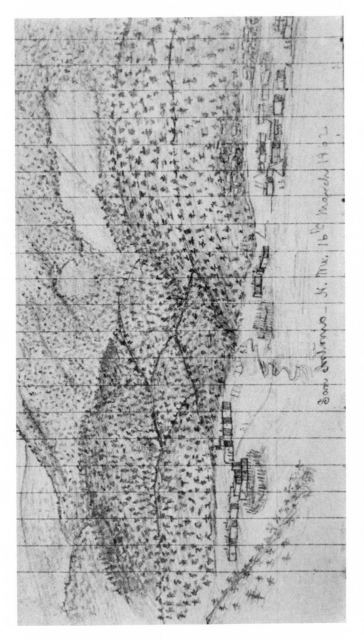

"San Antonio, N.M. 16th March 1862." Peticolas's sketch of the village on the eastern foot of the Sandia Mountains. The view is looking west toward South Sandia Peak from a point just east of N.M. Highway 14 at Cedar Crest. (Peticolas Journal)

San Antonio, N.M., within hearing of the singing going on at our chaplain's usual Sunday services. Nothing else of interest happened today. Spent my time reading.

Monday, 17 March 1862

Lying in camp and nothing unusual going on.

Tuesday and Wednesday; 18, 19 March 1862

Still lying in camp. Talk of our leaving soon; place of destination uncertain. 16 mules dead and more nearly so.

Thursday, 20 March 1862

Drew rations today. I read a good deal and worked on a drawing I am making of the battle of Val Verde. I draw the picture at the time of our making the charge on the right and left. More news of our leaving. Finished drawing rations for 10 days and worked on my picture. Nothing of importance going on in camp. Talk of leaving.

Friday, 21 March 1862

Took up the line of march today. Traveled 7 miles on towards Santa Fe and camped.[37] It being the 21st, we indulged in a good many remarks about the battle we fought today one month ago. As we came on, speculated upon the time when the war would end, pictured to each other our probable condition as individuals at the end of the war should it last 3 years, as now seems more than probable from the appearance of everything and the news we hear. I hope, however, it may sooner terminate in the recognition of the S.C. [Southern Confederacy] as an independent power by all nations.

Saturday, 22 March 1862

Laid in camp today. I amuse myself drawing, reading, and playing cards. Got some cough medicine for my cold this evening that did no good, but puked Williams. On picket guard tonight. Quartered in an old deserted ranch about ½ of a mile from camp down the road. We pulled down part of an off room of the ranch and made a

---

37. The First Regiment camped north of the village of San Antonito, near San Pedro Creek, while the Third Regiment remained behind to escort the supply wagons. Along with the command's sick, those companies of the Second Regiment that had gone into the Sandia Mountains returned to Albuquerque in order to oppose any movements by Federal troops from Fort Craig. (Hanna Journal, entries for 17, 20, 22 March 1862; O.R. IX: 509.)

good fire in the larger room. I had a magazine to read and did not suffer any inconvenience from being on guard.

Sunday, 23 March 1862

Traveled today 9 miles through one immense pinion country, rolling and mountains on every side. About 2 miles from camp we took a right-hand road, filled our canteens, and saw no more water till we reached camp.[38] The road turns almost at right angles to the course we have been pursuing and I think we are crossing the country to get to Ft. Union. The pine is low and scrubby, at least the most of it, but I have seen good timber trees through the country and can easily believe that fine timber can be procured in the gorges of the mountains.

Monday, 24 March 1862

Made quite an early start this morning, and our company being one of those in the advance, we traveled quite briskly. The country presents no features of peculiar interest, but is very much like what we have been traveling through for the last day or two. The mountain scenery in places is picturesque and interesting, but an air of desolate lonesomeness reigns over the whole country. No living thing can we see as we travel on, save animals and men accompanying us, and not even a bird flies across the road or chirrups in the bushes as we pass. We traveled 10 miles today and passed some old gold mines, or rather excavations, which do not appear to have rewarded the labor of the miners very well. We camped this evening at a little village in a mountain valley,[39] the principal feature of which is a large gold mill for crushing quartz, owned, it is said, by northern men. I got several specimens of quartz. Spent 1/2 an hour in the mill very pleasantly and hear that the yield here is from $100 to 300 $ per ton of quartz, and that the gold is worth 18 $ per oz. The quartz is crushed by huge beams that work up and down. It is a steam mill and the machinery must have cost a good deal. We got wood from the village and water from the mill tanks. About midday we were passing along the piney slope in the east side of the mountains, and through openings in the woods we could see a vast plain, not unlike the Journada del Muerte opposite Roblero. An immense valley ex-

---

38. Peticolas's camp was east of the mining town of Golden.

39. The village of Reál de Dolores is still the center of gold mining operations in the Ortiz Mountains.

Peticolas's sketch of the gold mill at Real de Dolores, near Galisteo, N.M. (Arizona Historical Society)

The church at Galisteo, 25 March 1862. (Arizona Historical Society)

tending from the foot of the range of mountains along which we were passing, to another far-off range in the distance could be seen, and I began to think that this was the valley of the Pecos, but no one has yet been able to inform me whether I was right or wrong in my conjecture.

Tuesday, 25 March 1862

We took up the line of march this morning at a reasonably early hour and traveled 4 miles down a long slope and out of the piney country. We then reached the valley and traveled a good distance over a first-rate road and camped 12 miles from the gold mines at Galisteo. This is a small town situated on a small creek of the same

74

name. We are now on one of the main roads from Craig to Union and considerably fatigued with our march. We were not sorry to know that we had at last reached a point where we could rest a little. [Lucius M.] Scott, Commissary Sgt., captured a large flock of sheep on the way and pressed them into service, as we are just now rather short of meat.

Wednesday, 26 March 1862

Laid over today and waited for the 3rd Regt. Towards evening it came in and two or three hours after, an express from Major Pyron came in informing us that he had been attacked by a large body of Pike's Peak men during the day; that he had gotten the best of the engagement and had fallen back to wood and water, which he would hold till we came up to him.[40] The order was immediately given,

---

40. After occupying Santa Fe for two weeks and being reinforced by four companies of the Second Regiment, Major Pyron learned that Federal forces from Fort Union were approaching the capital. Thereupon, the aggressive commander of Sibley's advance guard marched to meet his enemies in the mountains east of Santa Fe, where the constricted nature of the ground along the Santa Fe Trail would neutralize the Federals' anticipated numerical advantage. Pyron's force of approximately 400 men included his own battalion, the four Second Regiment companies, three locally recruited "spy companies," and artillerymen with two six-pounder field guns. The Federal forces advancing against the Texans were the First Colorado Volunteers, who had marched down from Denver City in rapid answer to Canby's request to that territory's governor, and units of regular infantry, cavalry, and artillery from Fort Union. Commanded by the First Colorado's colonel, John P. Slough, this field column numbered approximately 1,340 men and eight cannons. On the morning of 26 March 1862, Pyron's Texans marched eastward along the Santa Fe Trail, while Slough's advance guard, approximately 420 men under the command of Maj. John M. Chivington, First Colorado Volunteers, moved westward toward them on the same road. The Federals surprised and captured Pyron's small vanguard, then attacked his main body of troops. Forming in line of battle across the road approximately a mile west of Glorieta Pass, the Texans unlimbered their artillery and opened fire on the "Pike's Peakers" and regulars. The Union forces, however, outflanked Pyron's line by climbing the hillsides bordering the Santa Fe Trail. Thereupon, the Confederates withdrew westward toward Apache Canyon, a small valley of cultivated fields bisected by Apache Creek, and established a second, and probably a third, similar battleline. There Chivington repeated his outflanking tactic and, in addition, sent a furious cavalry charge by the only mounted company of the First Colorado against the Texan positions. Pyron managed to extract his two cannons, but the Union horsemen were among his infantry just as Chivington's flanking parties reached his rear. As a result, seventy Confederates were captured during this Battle of Apache Canyon, while approximately four Texans died and twenty were wounded. Pyron's report of these operations has never been located, so exact numbers cannot be determined; but the loss in prisoners of war was the greatest tactical defeat suffered by the Sibley Brigade during the New Mexico campaign. Pyron retreated to his supply train and camp at Cañoncito, near the western entrance to Apache Canyon. Expecting an attack by the

and in an hour after we received the express, we were all under way. This, however, made it about 8 o'clock when we started, and we were told that the distance we had to go was 12 miles, but before it was walked we found it to be at least 15. Pyron had two men killed and 3 wounded. The forces were about 350 on our side, 3 or 4 companies of the 2nd Regt, and from 600 to 1000 of the enemy. We started off at a brisk gait and made the first six miles of our journey in a very little time, but footsore and weary we did not travel from that point so fast as we had been doing, but there was no murmuring at our suffering, and on the want of comfort on this our forced march, but every man marched bravely along and did not complain at the length of the road, the coldness of the weather, or the necessity that compelled the march. We passed over a very steep pass in the mountains not far from a ranch buried in a circular valley in the bosom of the mountains, and as the ascent and descent was extremely difficult, we were nearly two hours crossing, and while the command was waiting for the artillery and ammunition wagons to cross over, they made large fires at the foot of the pass and warmed chilled hands and feet. About 1/2 past 3 we reached a ranch down the canion and were directed to get wood wherever we could and make fires.[41] Now we had no blankets, and Jones proposed to me to go and try and get into a house to sleep, which I succeeded in doing. He and I slept together on the floor with no bedding, and only a few articles of women's wearing apparel which we found scattered round the house.

Thursday, 27 March 1862

We went down a hundred yards or so this morning, and finding a very strong natural position, we halted in line and began to increase the elevation of the bank behind which we were to fight. In our front the road passed through a narrow opening between the

---

entire Federal force on the following day, he sent an urgent request for assistance to Scurry, camped fifteen miles away at Galisteo. Major Chivington, having lost five men killed and fourteen wounded, retired with his party and their prisoners to the main Union camp at Koslowski's Ranch, south of the village of Pecos. (*O.R.* IX: 530–31; Hollister, *Boldly They Rode*, pp. 61–67.)

41. Peticolas had reached Johnson's Ranch, located at Cañoncito. No traces of the ranch buildings remain, although several early photographs survive. Pyron's, and later, Scurry's, supply wagons were parked along Galisteo and Indian creeks, which join at Cañoncito. Their draft animals were held in side canyons nearby. This wagon park was the object of a severe Union attack two days later, during the Battle of Glorieta.

mountains. Behind us was a considerable hill bristling with our cannon, and on the sides of the mountains were placed our sharp shooters.[42] This very strong position they did not come to attack, and we laid here all day awaiting them. Our wagons got in about dinner time and we had a good supper, having eaten a dinner of sweetened mush, which we made from meal that we found at this ranch. Theodor Schultz, who had been ill 5 days with pneumonia, died last night, and we buried him today about three o'clock P.M. Poor boy, a stranger in a strange land, he sleeps the sleep that knows no waking.

Friday, 28 March 1862

We had been told by Col. Scurry that if the enemy did not come to us that we would go to them, so this morning we started for their camps 8 miles below us. Our company was ordered out on picket duty in the morning and remained out till the cannon had passed. Green, having received an express telling him of our situation, had promised to be at our camp by 12 today.[43] Fearing nothing for our train, we left it behind and marched out to give battle to our enemy about 5 miles below, where they were reported to be camped. When within about a mile of their camp, they suddenly made their appearance around a bend in the road about 250 yards off. Cannon were quickly unlimbered and the men aligned, but before they had all gained position, the sharp report of a gun and sharper whistle of a minie ball warned us that they had come out to meet us.[44] The

---

42. As the Santa Fe Trail emerged from the narrow entrance to Apache Canyon, following the bed of Galisteo Creek, it turned abruptly to pass through Cañoncito and Johnson's Ranch, then continued northwestward fifteen miles to Santa Fe. Commanding this narrow exit is a small hill on which the Texans placed their guns and dug earthworks for their infantry. During the Mexican War, New Mexico governor Manuel Armijo had fortified this same hill in anticipated, or feigned, resistance to the westward advance of Gen. Stephen W. Kearny.

43. This rumor undoubtedly boosted the morale of Scurry's men, but in fact, Green and the remaining companies of the Second Regiment were still at Albuquerque and were in no position to reinforce the more advanced Texans. Sibley was also still in Albuquerque.

44. These shots opened the Battle of Glorieta at about eleven o'clock. As had happened two days before, the opposing forces advanced toward one another along the Santa Fe Trail. The Texan advance guard encountered its Federal equivalent about one mile east of Glorieta Pass. Colonel Slough's main Union force was resting and filling canteens at Pigeon's Ranch, a half mile farther east. He had approximately 850 men available for the upcoming fight, including six companies of the First Colorado Volunteers, detachments from the First and Third U.S. Cavalry regiments, and

Col. John P. Slough, Col. John M. Chivington, commanders of the First Colorado Volunteers at the battles of Glorieta and Apache Canyon. (Colorado Historical Society)

road here down Apache Canion runs through a densely wooded pine country where you cannot see a man 20 steps unless he is moving. The hills slope up from the valley gradually, rising more abruptly as they near the mountains. Heavy masses of rock, too, crown most of these hills, and the timber is low and dense. On the left, the hills rise more abruptly than on the right and the rocks are larger. About a mile down the canion is Pidgeon's Ranch,[45] around which was the

two artillery batteries of four guns each, manned by regular cavalry and infantry soldiers. The balance of Slough's troops, approximately 490 men led by Major Chivington, had earlier left the main force to act as a flanking party. They had climbed Rowe Mesa, whose flat top bordered the Santa Fe Trail on the south and ran westward to end abruptly above the Confederate camp at Cañoncito. As the main battle opened, Chivington was pushing his men across the heavily wooded mesa toward an expected fight at the Texans' camp, unaware that the main forces had already met near Glorieta. In command of the Texan force, Lieutenant Colonel Scurry brought approximately 1,000 men onto the main battlefield. He thus slightly outnumbered his Federal opponents. The Confederates included nine companies of the First Regiment, four each of the Second and Third regiments, and Pyron's battalion. As artillery support, the Texans had three cannons manned by crews detailed from the various regiments of the Sibley Brigade. Although these have long been thought to be six-pounder field guns, the editor's artifact evidence indicates that at least one Confederate cannon was a twelve-pounder field howitzer. The initial Texan artillery and infantry support positions on the ridge just west of Windmill Hill were identified by the editor in 1979. (*O.R.* IX: 533–35, 538–39, 541–42.)

enemy's encampment. As soon as their infantry opened upon us, our Artillery began to play upon them, and we began to fire at intervals with our minie muskets as we could see an object to fire at. As usual, Co. C was directly in the rear of the cannon. On our right was an old field fenced in with pine poles. To this field a good many of us repaired when the firing grew hot, and shot at our enemy on the [Union] left. Presently the firing on the [Union] right began to be very rapid and hot, and soon we heard a cheer announcing that the enemy were retiring, as I found afterwards. Meantime, the firing upon our company and the artillery became so hot that the artillerymen could not stand it, and cutting out our horses that had been shot, they hastily limbered up and departed, leaving one man dead. Sam Brown was wounded here. Meantime, our men were steadily pressing in [on] the right, and to these I joined myself as soon as we left the fence. A party of our men were sent over on the left on the opposite mountain and we all fought the same way, advancing steadily from tree to tree and shooting at every enemy that showed himself. About this time the enemy was discovered in force in a deep gully in the old field on our left, or rather about the center of the Canion, and a charge was ordered upon them. Most of our Co. C was in this, but Lytle and myself, being almost on the extreme right, were not in it. Our boys dashed down upon them with a yell and plunging into the gully came to a hand-to-hand conflict with them. Capt. [Charles B.] Buckholts killed one with a bowie knife. He was killed himself later in the day. [Henry] Elliott, my informant, says that when they plunged into the gully, there were 13 men still remaining, the rest having fled. Of these, 6 were killed and 5 taken prisoners.[46] Our boys then took possession of this position and shot at the enemy on the left and down towards the ranch. We had pressed

---

45. Pigeon's Ranch was a major hostelry on the Santa Fe Trail. Built in 1851, the main adobe buildings were clustered on both sides of the road as it emerged from a narrow canyon formed by an abrupt, rocky ridge north of the ranch and a steep-sided hill to the south. Both these elevations, Sharpshooters Ridge and Artillery Hill, respectively, played key roles in the subsequent battle. An adobe wall, part of a large corral complex, ran across the mouth of the canyon just west of the ranch. The main building and well of Pigeon's Ranch still survive.

46. The Federal troops involved were men of Company I, First Colorado Volunteers, sent to outflank the Texan battleline on the north side of the Santa Fe Trail. The company's survivors retreated to large rock formations on the slopes that form the northern boundary of the Glorieta battlefield. There they became the extreme right flank of the Union line until driven from the position later in the battle. (*O.R.* IX: 542–43.)

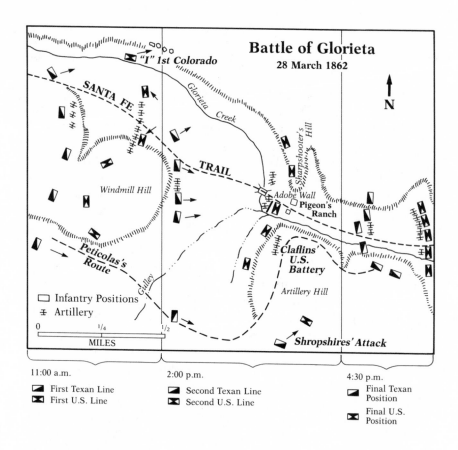

Battle of Glorieta
28 March 1862

N

"I" 1st Colorado

SANTA FE

Glorieta Creek

TRAIL

Sharpshooter's Hill

Windmill Hill

Adobe Wall

Pigeon's Ranch

Peticolas's Route

Gulley

Claflins' U.S. Battery

Artillery Hill

☐ Infantry Positions
✦ Artillery

0   ¼   ½
MILES

Shropshires' Attack

11:00 a.m.

◤ First Texan Line
◪ First U.S. Line

2:00 p.m.

◤ Second Texan Line
◪ Second U.S. Line

4:30 p.m.

◤ Final Texan Position

◪ Final U.S. Position

in their right and left up to this time equally rapidly, but after taking possession of a little eminence on the right, commanding the ranch and adobe Corralls in the valley, there was a temporary lull and our artillery was ordered up to tear the corralls in pieces from this eminence.[47] Major Pyron then came down to the right and ordered us further on to a little gully in the old field, while a force about 200 went up on the left. We laid in the gully on the right ¹/₂ an hour and then were ordered further on, and rapidly ascended another little eminence where the enemy had their artillery ¹/₂ an hour before,[48] when a perfect hail of grape-shot came tearing the trees and brushing the brow of the hill and making a tremendous noise, but fortunately without hurting any body. We soon passed this hill and began to descend again and to spread out to the right, firing at the enemy whenever visible. This was about 3 o'clock in the evening and we had been pushing them back all day. I now got on the brow of the hill and began to shoot down in the valley at the enemy in the valley on the right. I saw the *Abs* run on the left and our men pressing on. Then I heard the men in the gully in the old field give a shout and come running down towards the ranch in the valley, and then the [Federal] artillery opened upon them with grape and canister, and they all began to find some safe place behind the Corralls and houses and trees. We on the right were a good distance below the ranch on the hill, and now [if] we could flank them on the right and drive back the party that was holding us in check; their battery was ours.[49]

---

47. The eminence to which Peticolas refers is today called Windmill Hill. The initial Federal battleline was along its northern and western slopes. Major Pyron, commanding the Texan right, successfully pushed around the southern slopes of Windmill Hill, with Peticolas as part of his force. Outflanked, and under steady pressure from the Confederate center, about two o'clock Slough withdrew his troops some 800 yards, establishing a second battleline immediately in front of Pigeon's Ranch. The eastern face of Windmill Hill then became the center of the second Confederate line when Scurry established his headquarters there.

48. Capt. John F. Ritter's battery of two twelve-pounder field howitzers and two six-pounder field guns had earlier occupied this slight ridge near the southern edge of the battlefield. The position is now beneath the roadbed of Interstate 25. Ritter withdrew to Pigeon's Ranch as his cannons came under fire from Pyron's advancing Texans. (*O.R.* IX: 539–40.)

49. Peticolas, with the other men of the Confederate right, had advanced to a point just south of Interstate 25 and were facing the western and southern slopes of Artillery Hill, so named because Lieutenant Ira W. Claflin's battery of four twelve-pounder mountain howitzers fired on the Texans from a position near its summit early in the battle. By the time Peticolas charged the hill, however, Claflin had moved the howitzers to a position near the Santa Fe Trail and Pigeon's Ranch, the center of the Union line. (*O.R.* IX: 536, 539–40.)

About the time the severest fighting was going on on the left and the men were charging in the center, Major Shropshire ordered us to a charge on the right in a right oblique motion so as to get past their left and succeed in driving them back.[50] And now came the severest fight that we on the right had during the day. We charged up a hill with a wide seam of fair open ground to cross on, towards an enemy who were hidden and invisible and who waited patiently for us to approach to shoot us down. Up we went, taking advantage of every bush and tree to shelter us, and before we had crossed the opening, more than 2/3 rds of the men had stopped, fearing to go into it, but 35 or 40 brave souls, led on by Col. Scurry, Major [John S.] Shropshire, Capt. Buckholts, and Capt. [James M.] Odell, went, and all the men in Co. C on the right went in this charge. We saw no foe till in twenty yards of them, and then they rose from behind their breast works of rocks and poured into us a deadly volley.

Now I must tell just here of a very singular accident that befell me. I was in the extreme left of the charging party and in fact on the very verge of the hill. The undergrowth was thick and I did not see that Major Shropshire, Capt. Buckholts, and 3 men had been killed by the firing I heard on my right, nor hear that Scurry had ordered the men to fall back. The men having obliqued to the right, the firing at the point where I approached their line was very slight, so that when I ceased [advancing], I thought that the enemy had been forced back by our men and that they had taken out toward the hills, as I thought the firing seemed to tend in that direction. So not desiring to follow in that direction, but having an excellent chance to fire across in the valley at the artillerymen and on the left, I began to take part in the battle again by walking leisurely along the hill towards where their line was, firing at every opportunity down at the enemy.[51] I was thus slowly advancing, and after

---

50. Scurry planned a coordinated attack against the strong Union lines. He sent Major John S. Shropshire to lead the Texan right against the Artillery Hill positions held by Colorado infantrymen. Majors Pyron and Raguet led the Confederates on the left against the Colorado and regular troops holding the line along Sharpshooter's Ridge, north of Pigeon's Ranch. Scurry commanded the center, which charged directly at the massed Federal artillery and infantry supports on and near the Santa Fe Trail. This plan went awry when Major Shropshire was killed and the right-flank assault, in which Peticolas participated, failed. Repeated attacks in the center also failed, but the Texans were successful in getting onto Sharpshooter's Ridge above Pigeon's Ranch and driving off its Union defenders. Once they had done so, the Federal artillery positions near Pigeon's Ranch were untenable, and the guns were limbered up and withdrawn eastward along the road to a final battleline near the present-day Confederate monument. (*O.R.* IX: 537–38, 540, 544.)

having fired $\frac{1}{2}$ a dozen shots thus, was loading my gun when on turning $\frac{1}{2}$ around, and to my astonishment, saw that I was in two feet of a line of 100 men, all strangers to me. Another glance as I returned ramming convinced me that they were Pikes Peakers and in a moment I thought, well, I'm a prisoner after all. Here are the enemy. Before I could act upon this conviction; in fact before I had decided what to do with 50 men looking at me and possessing the power to riddle me with pistol balls or minie balls or plunge a bayonet in me—the major of the enemy nearest me, a man with a red band cap, dark eyes and whiskers and rather handsome face, height 5 ft 10 in, said, looking straight into my face, "you had better look out, Capt., or those fellows will shoot you."[52] Now though I knew that he referred to our men and mistook me for some on his own side, I felt puzzled to say anything save to look inquiringly at him and ask, "Who will?" My voice did not betray that 50 men were looking at me and none of them by word or sign showed that he knew me in my true character. He answered, "Why, those fellows over yonder," pointing in the direction of our boys. "There are two or three of them over there shooting at us." "Is there," said I; "Then I'll go over that way and take a shot at them." I started off with my gun at charge bayonets, walking cautiously, taking advantage of the trees as if advancing on a real foe, and as I thus walked off, I looked anew over my shoulder at the man who had been talking to me. He was watching me very closely and I felt some uneasiness lest he should shoot me in the back as I went off, but his honest eyes looked no suspicion, and in a dozen steps further I was out of sight and over in our own lines once more. I felt joyous that I was not a prisoner and thanking an overriding Providence for my escape.

In a few moments we all got together again and advanced

---

51. When Claflin's battery left this area earlier, the infantry supporting the artillerymen left also, creating a large gap in the Union line. Peticolas walked through this gap and along the northern rim of Artillery Hill, overlooking Pigeon's Ranch and the center of the Federal line. The Colorado Volunteers on Artillery Hill had beaten off Shropshire's attack, then fallen back to the next slope east of Artillery Hill to shorten their lines and await the next Texan assault. This position, and Claflin's battery location, were identified through artifact evidence by the editor in 1980.

52. The officer who addressed Peticolas was probably Lt. Col. Samuel F. Tappan, First Colorado Volunteers, commanding the southern half of the Union line. No Federal major was present on the field, and the insignia of rank for major and lieutenant colonel were very similar. Tappan's excellent report of the battle, however, makes no mention of such an incident. Peticolas was apparently wearing the Federal overcoat he had acquired at the Battle of Valverde a month earlier, and was thus mistaken for a Union officer.

Lt. Col. Samuel F. Tappan, First Colorado
Volunteers. Tappan commanded the left
of the Union line at Glorieta, opposing
the Texans with whom Peticolas fought.
He failed to recognize Peticolas as an
enemy during the later stage of the
battle. (Colorado Historical Society)

towards the enemy, for I had informed Capt. Crosson, Commanding,
of my visit to their lines and their force, etc. When we got to our
wounded and dead, we found that there was no enemy there; they
had left the field and were retreating rapidly, having gotten off with
Cannon and train. This was the last of the battle.[53] We rallied in

---

53. After the encounter with Peticolas, Tappan realized that the Union forces to
his north had withdrawn and that the Rebels had occupied Pigeon's Ranch and the
former Federal positions around it with infantry and two pieces of artillery. To avoid
being cut off, he quickly evacuated his position and fell back to the final Union line.
The Confederates followed, and both sides exchanged desultory cannon and small-
arms fire. This effort died out in mutual exhaustion, and Slough decided to withdraw
to his camp at Kozlowski's Ranch, some five miles to the rear. Scurry was thus left
in possession of the battlefield. He and his men felt they had won a considerable
victory, although in fact little had been gained, and losses were almost the same as

force further down on the road and began to follow the retreating foe, but just about the time that we were well on the way after them, news came that a detachment of the enemy's Cavalry had passed round through the mountains and attacked, taken, and burnt our train. We heard cannonading in our rear about this time and did not know what to think of it. But it turned out in fact that they had burned our train and then retreated rapidly, half frightened to death for fear of our return before they got away.[54]

The battle began at 10 minutes to 11 and ended about 4 o'clock. We had 35 killed and 33 wounded. They had from 60 to 100 killed and from 1 to 300 wounded.[55] Of our company, A.[lexander] Montgomery, Jake [Jacob] Henson, and Abe Hanna were killed; [Samuel]

those suffered by the Federals. The Union troops also felt they had been successful and were being unjustly kept from renewing the fight. Whatever the actual result on the main battlefield (and a draw seems the most reasonable evaluation), a strong, undefeated Federal force still stood between the Texans and their objective, Fort Union. (*O.R.* IX: 537–38; Hollister, *Boldly They Rode*, pp. 72, 74.)

54. It cannot be definitely determined whether this news stopped the fighting or whether it ended, as Scurry reported, because of "the extreme exhaustion of the men, who had been engaged for six hours in the hardest contested fight it has ever been my lot to witness." However, as the battle raged around Pigeon's Ranch, Major Chivington's party, guided by Lt. Col. Manuel A. Chavez, Second New Mexico Volunteers, reached the western bluffs of Rowe Mesa at a point some 200 feet directly above the Texan's wagon park and camp near Johnson's Ranch and Cañoncito. Finding no battle in progress there, as they had expected, the Federal troops descended the steep slopes above the Confederate encampment, drove off the weak wagon guard, captured and disabled the one cannon left at the site, and burned and destroyed the entire eighty-wagon supply train. In it was virtually everything Scurry's force owned— reserve ammunition, baggage, food, forage, and medicines. After freeing a party of Union soldiers who had just been captured at Pigeon's Ranch, and learning for the first time of that fighting, the Federals retraced their steps up the hillside and back toward their old camp at Kozlowski's Ranch, where they rejoined Slough's main force after dark. Intended as a standard Napoleonic assault, Chivington's flanking *manoeuvre sur les derrières* was supposed to be coordinated with Slough's main attack on the Confederates with the Union *masse de décision*. Such tactics were common knowledge as the Civil War began and looked attractive to inexperienced commanders such as Slough. Generally, however, amateur soldiers were unable to execute anything so complex, especially in the heavily wooded mountains of New Mexico. Nevertheless, this phase of the Battle of Glorieta was a resounding strategic victory and made Sibley's eventual defeat inevitable. (*O.R.* IX: 538–39, 544; Geisecke Diary, entry for 28 March 1862; Marc Simmons, *The Little Lion of the Southwest: A Life of Manuel Antonio Chavez* [Chicago: Sage Books, 1973], pp. 183–85.)

55. The Confederates actually lost thirty-six killed and sixty wounded, with about two-thirds of the losses coming from the First Regiment. In addition, they had about twenty-five men captured. Federal losses at Glorieta are less exactly known, but were about thirty-eight killed, sixty-four wounded, and twenty captured. (*O.R.* IX: 535, 537–38, 545.)

Brown, [Cpl. Lovell J.] Bartlett, and [Benjamin N.] White wounded. All our killed were shot in the very front of the battle. Abe Hanna was shot down on the left in 30 yards of the enemy. Jake Henson, who was on the same side, coming along and seeing Abe down, went to him, gave him water, and began to pick the stones from under him. While in a kneeling position over his wounded friend he was shot and killed, the ball going in at the shoulder and ranging towards the heart. Abe Hanna died about an hour in the night very easily. He was shot in the loins and bled inwardly. He said he felt no pain save that his limbs were numb and dead from his hips down. Monte was killed in the valley in the very front of the charge. Thus ended the battle of Glorietta Valley, in which we gained a complete victory but at the expense of every comfort. We passed over the battlefield in the evening looking for the wounded, and I was taken by a wounded Pike's Peak man to whom I stopped to converse with, for one of his own men; also by a Sergeant of the artillery who came back to look up the wounded and bury the dead. They had run clear off. 3/4 of an hour had elapsed since all firing had ceased, and they made no effort to get permission to bury their dead. So Col. Scurry sent Maj. Pyron back with a flag of truce, informing them that he granted them permission to return and bury their dead and take off their wounded, as his men were too tired to do it for them. News then came down to us that Col. Green had arrived in the Canion behind us and had engaged the enemy who had captured our baggage train, and we were ordered out back towards our old encampment to cut off their retreat should they come down the canion. We got some dried buffalo beef at a ranch a little back where the Abs had it stored and we lined our haversacks pretty bountifully with it. I was on guard to-night and was up for the night. We were on picket up the road towards our old camp and when my turn was out, I curled up by the fire wrapped up in my overcoat and managed to get a few hours' repose. I was very thankful that I had no depression of Spirits or many nervous feelings after the battle as I had at *Val Verde*, for I should have been unfit for guard duty if I had felt as I felt that night.

Saturday, 29 March 1862

We ate a morsel of dried beef this morning and moved on up towards our old camp with the part of the Command which was an outpost under Capt. Naughton. Then we went into Camp while the rest of the men were busy burying the dead and attending to the wounded. We learned certainly before noon that our baggage train had been all burnt and that the Mexicans were busy stealing every thing they could lay their hands on. Green had not come as reported, and so our things were indeed destroyed. I didn't mind losing any-thing save my watch and journal—that I cared much about losing.[56] We got mutton today for dinner; a flock of sheep belonging to some one in the Canion. We learned today that most of the men who were at the wagons escaped and went to Santa Fe. [C. B.] Callendar and [Gideon] Egg were taken prisoners and John [A.] Warburton was supposed to be killed; he is certainly either killed or taken prisoner, and [Sgt. Lucius M.] Scott also is taken. We had taken some 10 or 15 prisoners and sent them back to the wagons. They were retaken. We have now, however, 20 left. Towards night we were ordered to prepare for marching orders, and an express came in from Santa Fe to Scurry, the nature of which I did not learn. About 10 P.M. we were ordered to get our guns to march and the rest of the command coming up, we took up the line of march for Santa Fe. Marched all night; distance about 22 miles. We reached a small creek about 4 A.M. and stopped an hour to wait for those that had given out on the road and stopped to rest. The timber on the road is pine, large and tall; the road is good, and gradually ascends for 14 miles, when it reaches the height of the range of hills over which it passes and then gradually descends till it reaches the creek at which we stopped. From thence it skirts along the mountains for four miles and de-scends to Santa Fe. Like a good many of our company, I expected to stop at these fires, get a nap, and wait for day to make the rest of the distance. I was perfectly worn out and soon fell asleep and slept by the fire till day.

Sunday, 30 March 1862

We walked into Santa Fe today. I gazed down with feelings of curiosity and interest at this the oldest city in the territory, from the height of the hills on the south of the city. The church spires glittered in the light of the morning sun, and the multitude of one-story adobe buildings looked neat and comforable to us worn and footsore soldiers.[57] The town is laid out with some degree of regu-

---

56. Peticolas refers to volume one of his three Civil War journals, which was burned along with whatever other baggage he had in the wagon train parked at Johnson's Ranch.

57. From Santa Fe's Loretto Academy, Mother Madgalen Hayden observed:

They continued entering until almost noon on Sunday: We could hear

larity and though not so large as I thought it was, is still a place of considerable importance, being the capital of the territory. Women in their long shawls wrapped about their heads and faces were filling their water jugs at the little canal that we first crossed as we entered town. A few copper-colored citizens were lounging on the corners, and one old fellow with a cane and cloak was walking briskly up the street, but these were all the persons that we saw stirring. We stopped at a store about ½ way to our quarters and got some bread and whiskey, for which [W. T.] Davis and myself payed coffee that we had gotten at Johnson's Ranch, where our things were burnt. Further on we met a crowd of boys spinning tops and enjoying themselves considerably to all appearances. We found our quarters in a large old ruined building belonging to the government, and about 12 M. got rations and dinner. We slept in this house on hay from the Government Corralls. The following is a copy of the address that Col. Scurry issued to the men under his command as soon as he could get it printed (further on).

Monday, 31 March 1862

Laid in camps today. Wandered over town looking at it. Companies are securing better quarters than they have in the old ruined government buildings. The quartermasters and commissary department are hard at work preparing to supply our wants in the clothing and blanket line. 30,000 $ worth of government property have been found. The company of Santa Fe Gamblers who joined us since the battle of *Val Verde* and fought gallantly and desperately at Glorietta, is of immense service to us now. They call themselves *brigands* and know everything about Santa Fe. Mrs. Canby [wife of the Federal commander] is in this city and visits the hospital regularly to wait on the sick of both sides. We heard here that Gov. Conway [Connelly] was at Glorieta and promised the men that they should have a ball in Santa Fe tonight. They were 1800 strong and

---

them passing all night, our convent being on the street through which they had to pass, but we did not know to which side they belonged until morning when we saw by their clothes that they were Texans. Some came on horseback, others on foot, and others were almost dragged to the city. All were in a most needy and destitute condition in regard to the commonest necessities of life. . . . We hid many of our provisions for fear they would pay us a visit when they found no more in other places. (Mother Magdalen Hayden to "Sister," 7 May 1862, in Straw, *Loretto,* pp. 35–36, 38.)

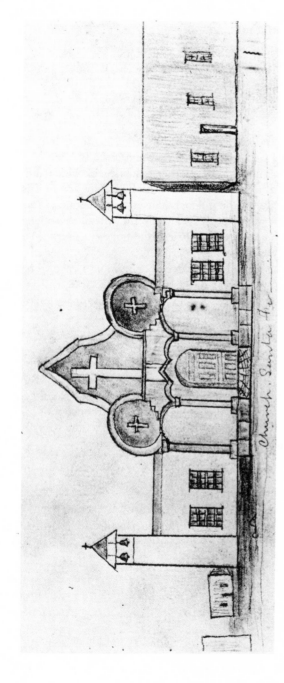

"Church, Santa Fe." Sketch by an unknown Texan soldier, later copied by Peticolas. (Arizona Historical Society)

certain of success, but they had reason to experience the truth of that old saw, "There's many a slip twixt the cup and the lip."

Here's Scurry's address:

Head-Quarters, Advance Division, Army of New Mexico
Canon Glorieta, March 29, 1862

General Order
No. 4

Soldiers:—You have added another victory to the long list of triumphs won by the Confederate *armies*. By your conduct, you have given another evidence, of the daring courage and heroic endurance, which actuate you in this great struggle for the independence of your country. You have proven your right to stand by the side of those who fought and conquered on the red field of San Jacinto. The battle of Glorieta—where for six long hours you steadily drove before you a foe of twice your numbers—over a field chosen by themselves, and deemed impregnable, will take its place upon the roll of your country's triumphs, and serve to excite your children to imitate the brave deeds of their fathers, in every hour of that country's peril. —Soldiers—I am proud of you. Go on as you have commenced, and it will not be long until not a single soldier of the United States will be left on the soil of New Mexico. The Territory, relieved of the burdens recently imposed upon it by its late oppressors, will once more, throughout its beautiful valleys, "blossom as the rose," beneath the plastic hand of peaceful industry.

By order of Lieut. Colonel W. R. SCURRY, Commanding
Ellsberry R. Lane, Adjutant

From all I can hear of San Jacinto, that battle was not near such a hotly contested fight as the battle of Glorietta or Val Verde either. This is the only fault I have to find with the address.

Tuesday, 1 April 1862

We have gotten quarters in a larger block of buildings belonging to the bishop, who is friendly to us.[58] Col. Scurry is *pro tem* Governor,

---

58. This was Bishop John B. Lamy. The block of buildings to which Peticolas refers was directly across the street to the northwest of the cathedral and was composed of single-story adobe dwellings, since torn down. The location has been identified by Mary Jean Cook of Santa Fe.

and Capt. Hampton Commander of the regiment. [R. G.] Purcell's mess and mine occupy one room with a good floor and fireplace. We are resting, but have very poor eating; no bacon nor pork, and very little coffee. I have seen very few American ladies as yet.[59]

Wednesday, 2 April 1862

Still lying up refitting. Drew a blanket apiece; got an order and did a little trading with a merchant who is friendly to us and sells to us. Living on corn meal. Cooking utensils are very scarce. Like all Catholic towns, this one abounds in bells, and it is not very harmonious to hear them all chiming for matins and vespers mornings and evenings, for they do not chord by any means, but the noise is rather disagreeable than otherwise, but there is nothing more inspiring than to hear *one* of these bells "sprinkling with holy sounds the air," their deep solemn tones ringing through the valley in which the town is situated. They bring recollections thronging to my mind, memories of the long-gone time when I, a little fellow clinging to Mother's black-kidded hand and carrying a hymnbook, walked slowly up the carpeted aisle of old Tab Street Church, Petersburg, Va. It recalls thronging crowds of friendly faces familiar to me in my juvenile years, faces which I see no more, faces that have passed away in the mists of departed years, never more to be seen on the pathway marked out for me. Santa Fe possesses some rich historic associations, but I have as yet seen no spot famous in the memoirs of the past. I am comfortable as far as a place to rest is concerned, but there is a sort of gloom resting on the company. We have lost three companions who were very dear to all of us, and though a soldier's life is calculated to render a man properly callous, it will be long

---

59. Peticolas may have seen few "American ladies," but other soldiers were not so reticent. Mother Hayden reported:

> The Texans had their quarters all around us. Some of them climbed on the roof of the day school and one entered the school itself through a window which looks out over the street, asking if the room was unoccupied. He opened another window which opens on the courtyard, but as soon as he saw some Sisters he went out the street window. . . . I sent for the Bishop and he notified the commander and so they ceased to molest us. (Mother Magdalen Hayden to "Sister," 7 May 1862, in Straw, *Loretto*, p. 38.)

These activities were considered rather droll once the members of Company C returned to Victoria. A descendant of Private A. Goldman remembered hearing stories of considerable kidding of those involved with looking over the convent wall at the nuns. ("Walk Home Long One," *Victoria Advocate*, 28 April 1983.)

before we forget Henson, Hanna, and Montgomery. We seldom sing now save when liquor abounds, and the sound of a violin makes me sad. We once had a fiddler but he is not ——. I had my first book of my journal burned by the Abs and have had to resort to a very abridged account of our trip across the plains drawn off from mine by J. F. Henson in a very small book. This I am copying into a larger book than this as fast as I can.[60] I employ all my leisure time this way. We can get books to read by borrowing them.

Thursday, 3 April 1862

The *abs* retreated from the Glorieta Valley 8 miles the evening of the battle. On the same night that we moved, they pulled up stakes and retreated 40 miles towards Union and commenced fortifying.

Col. Hopkins, the merchant with whom I traded, is a Virginian and a very clever man. He has loaned us books to read and traded with us and in every way showed that he is a friend. There are some merchants in this town, however, smooth-faced Jews, that are our bitter enemies and will not open their stores or sell on confederate paper. These ought to have all their property confiscated and ought to be run off from town themselves.

An exchange of prisoners, I heard, has been effected, and we may expect to see Callender, Scott, Egg, and Warburton, so says report. I am going to get some drawing paper if we stay here any length of time and take sketches in and around town. The houses in Santa Fe, though altogether built of adobes, are of a better sort than any I have yet seen. They are large and high-pitched, being on an average from 12 to 20 feet. The walls of the room in which we are quartered are 4 feet thick, windows of glass, and a deep recess and window sill making a first-rate table, and in fact large and deep enough for one man to lounge and read in. I am beginning to be a convert to the Mexican style of building. Let me describe the block in which we live, and I will describe the universal mode of building adopted by the citizens of the territory with the exception of a few American settlers. One long low building, say 15 ft. high by 20 to 40 broad, runs parallel to their streets that intersect at right angles. On the fourth side of the square, usually upon the most quiet street, is a large gateway with a smaller door set in it that, with an adobe

---

60. The editor has been unable to locate this abridgement. The soldier who copied Peticolas's diary was apparently Jacob Henson, recently killed at Glorieta.

wall continuation of the building, surrounds and shuts in a court yard. Now if the building is upon a business street, there are usually doors opening upon the street, and windows, and the store room runs back from the street, communicating with the inside courtyard if at all by a side passage. Perhaps doors open from private apartments upon this passage, but access to a private room do not very frequently open [on] the street, though windows do. Running parallel with the house and overhanging the street is a long piazza with ground or pavement of the street for floor. The long building which forms this house then has large gates or doors opening upon the street and a passage leading to the court within. If more rooms are desired, wings are built back into the court yard, usually with two rooms, divided by another passage which passes directly through it. Then if another wing is thrown out from the other face building, there is a smaller yard formed and sometimes an adobe wall forms the fourth side of this inner courtyard. Within this court are built the large bake ovens in which they cook, of an oval form and made of earth. The ground is pierced and wells dug and hen houses built within, and all the domestic affairs of a household conducted away from the scrutinizing gaze of strangers or criticizing neighbors. Sometimes there is quite a little population and different families dwelling within one of these squares. Then, does Mrs. C wish to chat a while with Mrs. B, all she has to do is to slip a long shawl over head and run across a court yard, open a door, thread a passage or two, and she is sitting cosily with her friend, without having to cross a street or turn a corner with masculine acquaintance ogling her through cold, scrutinizing opera glasses or envious neighbor wives noting the color and size and fit and texture, etc., of her outfit, to find material for the next dish of scandal to set out to visitors.

Now I am on guard tonight and am employing my leisure writing. This will account for my long-windedness on this subject. The guard house is in the Santa Fe Fire Co. room, in which are various and sundry articles used by firemen, though of what use a fire company is in a city built of mud I can't well see, and I think the poor scared US troops must have had a deal of trouble to render the destruction of the government buildings as complete as they did. But to the room. There is a black flag on one side plastered up against the wall with the inscription upon it in poorly done guilt [*sic*] letters: "Santa Fe Fire Comp'y, Instituted March 1860." Then there are several ladders lying around, a log table upon which they discussed their bread and cheese doubtless, a formidable row of buckets under the bench upon which I am writing, that runs along the wall, one pick axe, and two or three tin horns. Then there are large basket-shaped things, the utility of which I am at a loss to know, made of cloth and inscribed both in english and spanish upon every side, informing every one who chooses to examine them that: *"George Washington!!! The father of our country!!!!! First in War!!! First in Peace,* and*!!!!! First in the hearts of his Countrymen!!!!"*—at which astounding name and astonishing declaration, strange to say, no one appears surprised. But I wander. Let me sketch a little. Here's the flag. Below the flag I have drawn a plan of the block in which we are quartered. The black [hatching] represents the buildings, the white the courts and passages. Col. Green got in today.[61]

Friday, 4 April 1862

Still lying in quarters. Clothes are being gotten together and distributed to the companies who lost everything in the battle. I am on guard duty today.

Saturday, 5 April 1862

The 2nd Regiment came in last night. I saw [Sgt. James F.] Coffee and [James H.] Armstrong and a good many of our boys from Albikirque. They report everything quiet below. Canby at Craig is getting very short of rations and, rumor says, has left the fort, de-stroyed everything he had, and gone across the mountains with pack mules.[62] A small party of [Capt. Bethel] Coopwood's men from Me-silla have found a safe road round Craig, 40 miles east [west] of it and came up to us. The news from the states is a mixture of good

---

61. Upon learning of Scurry's plight following the Battle of Glorieta, Sibley and Green, with the remaining six companies of the Second Regiment and Teel's artillery, left Albuquerque for Santa Fe. The two commanders arrived in the capital ahead of their mounted troopers, who only averaged about twelve miles per day riding north-ward. (Howell Journal, entries for 1, 5 April 1862; Smith Journal, pp. 140–41.)

62. This rumor was only partially true. Rations at Fort Craig were indeed short and Canby had indeed left the post. Leaving Colonel Carson with the equivalent of one regiment of New Mexico Volunteers to hold Fort Craig, Canby marched northward on 1 April at the head of 1,210 regulars and volunteers, including four cannons of the reconstituted McRae's Battery, commanded by Lt. Joseph M. Bell. In the mean-time, Canby ordered Col. Gabriel R. Paul, commanding Fort Union, to leave a vol-unteer garrison at that post and march south to meet Canby's force somewhere near Albuquerque. On 6 April, Paul left Fort Union with about 1,200 of the regulars and Colorado Volunteers who had recently fought at Glorieta, bypassing that battlefield and retracing in reverse the route followed by Peticolas and his companions two weeks before. (O.R. IX: 549–50, 552; Hollister, *Boldly They Rode*, pp. 78–89.)

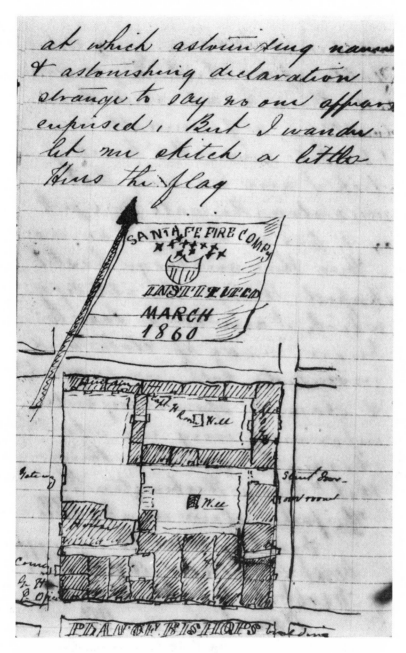

at which astounding names & astonishing declaration strange to say no one appeared surprised. But I wander, let me sketch a little this the flag

SANTA FE FIRE COMP.
INSTITUTED
MARCH
1860

Peticolas's sketch of the Santa Fe Fire Company flag and the block in which he was quartered, across the street northwest of the cathedral. (Peticolas Journal)

and bad. On the 2nd of March, so it goes, the Federal party lost a great battle on the Potomac, but by maneuvering they have taken Nashville, Tennessee, and even penetrated as far as Huntsville, Ala. Rumor, generally not believed, is current, too, that there has been landed at Aransas Bay 12,000 troops to over run Texas. They will have a merry time of it.

Sunday, 6 April 1862

The early chime of bells this morning tells us that the day of rest has come again. I sallied out this morning for a stroll with Davis, and we went into the Church next to us here. There are quite a number of pictures hanging upon the walls representing the sufferings and death, crucifixion and interment of Christ, very poorly done. One or two of the pictures are pretty good oil paintings. The furniture of the altar is very neat indeed and costly, but the seats are indifferent and scarce. Last night the boys had a Fandango in our room. I went in and looked on a while but did not take part. Yesterday, too, I visited a steam mill and saw some very good white wheat, the first I have seen since I left Va., grinding rapidly when I visited it.

Monday, 7 April 1862

Laid over today but received orders to leave this evening at 5 P.M. and we got ready but did not leave. There is a fandango tonight and all the boys and our Bill James and myself have gone to it. The understanding is that we leave tomorrow. Green's regiment left today at 12 M. for Alburquerque. We hear that Canby is approaching Albikirque with a considerable force.[63]

---

63. The Confederates had left a small garrison, two companies with three or four pieces of artillery, about 200 men, to guard their supply depot at Albuquerque. Although Canby's intentions as he approached that town have been a subject of heated debate, his subsequent actions seem to make them clear in retrospect. He could easily overpower the enemy at Albuquerque, even though he did not know their exact composition or strength. Having done so, his junction with Paul's column from Fort Union would have given him significant numerical superiority over Sibley's force. If Canby had wanted to meet and defeat the Texans in another major battle, he could have done so by advancing toward Santa Fe, maintaining a clear line of supply and communication with Fort Union. Instead, he had decided to draw the Rebels southward out of Santa Fe by threatening their supply depot at Albuquerque, to join with Paul's command in the Sandia Mountains east of that town, and thereafter to harry the Confederates southward out of New Mexico. He apparently felt that objective was consistent with his inability to feed and care for large numbers of prisoners should he defeat and capture Sibley's brigade. His approach to Albuquerque from

Tuesday, 8 April 1862

We made all our preparations this morning for a move, and having gotten some drawing paper yesterday from [Lt. Philip] Fulcrod, I today went down to old Hopkins and bought a large portfolio to keep my paper, pens, and ink in, and drawing paper. About 12 M. we left town, but not in order by any means, as the order was to leave scattering. About 2 hours after we started we all got together on the valley road to Alberquerque and in spite of new shoes and long rest we marched rapidly, but towards night the wagon guard got very strong, and I was one of them as my feet were *sore* indeed. We traveled 15 miles and camped on a small stream and took down a plank fence for wood. The night was cold but fatigue caused us to sleep soundly.

Wednesday, 9 April 1862

Express reached us last night that the *Abs* had attacked Alberquerque and been repulsed by [Captains] Hardeman and Coopwood, and that if we would hurry up we might take them all prisoners.[64] So off we started after a daybreak breakfast and marched till 10 P.M., 30 miles, and Oh the suffering of this march words can never tell. Footsore and weary we dragged along toward the river, reached the Rio Grande, whose yellow waters looked familiar as the face of an old friend to us, and then away down the sandy valley some 10 miles. Numbers we would pass on the road lying flat on the ground, entirely given out. Many clung to the wagons and sat on the tongues to get a little rest. Late at night, Sam Hyatt and myself fell together

---

the south had the desired effect, and the Second Regiment led the evacuation of Santa Fe only two days after its arrival there. (*O.R.* IX: 550–51; Capt. Jacob Downing and Pvt. John D. Howland, First Colorado Volunteers, "On the Gory Field of Glorieta Heights," *Santa Fe New Mexican*, 7 August 1906.)

64. During the previous afternoon, Canby reached Albuquerque and sent a small force to develop the strength of its defenders. A brief skirmish (often referred to as the Battle of Albuquerque) developed between opposing artillery units, resulting in one Union casualty. The firing ceased when Canby was informed that noncombatants in the town were endangered and were not permitted to leave by the Texans. His objective was being met, however, since the defenders immediately sent for assistance from Sibley and Green, thus hastening and making certain the evacuation of Santa Fe. Canby continued his feint against Albuquerque during 9 April with continued skirmishing, then withdrew eastward through Tijeras Canyon after dark. On 13 April, at San Antonio, the same small village in the Sandia Mountains where Peticolas had camped a month earlier, Canby united his force with that from Fort Union, giving him a field column of slightly more than 2,400 men. (*O.R.* IX: 550; Starr Campaign Letters, p. 179; Ickis Diary, entries for 9, 10 April 1862.)

and dragged along the road. Our company was in the rear guard today and all stragglers fell behind the whole command. We went on together till we got to a fire in the road and utterly exhausted we stopped here to take a nap. After we had slept an hour on the cold damp ground (for it had been snowing heavily in the mountains and some in the valleys during the day) we got up and walked on 2 miles further to camp, which was at Algerdonus [Algodones]. During the evening passing down the valley of the river we saw peach orchards in full bloom and the snow pouring down in the mountains. There is a high pass about 3 miles from the point where the road strikes the river valley, and from the top of it we could see the distant fire which we took for our camp fires, and from this point that blaze was our beacon star. How great then was our disappointment when we got there with wet feet and blistered, and tired sore legs, and eyes full of dust, and stomachs empty, and found that there was no camp there. (Sam and I had gotten our feet wet in trying to jump across a *saco* [*acéquia:* irrigation ditch] about 4 feet wide). I am rather surprised at our hardihood in attempting anything like a jump at all.

Thursday, 10 April 1862

It rained last night quite hard and our blankets were wet with this rain this morning. My cold is a good deal worse than it has been for some time. After we had gotten breakfast and our wagons loaded we started again, not however with the expectation of walking as far as we had done the day before, for it is not in the power of human endurance. Today was very cold and it was snowing all day. We passed through 3 or 4 towns on the river, at one of which we stopped to get forage. The men got something to eat, too, and a barrel of wine was broached by one of the wild boys. The wine was first rate and a great many of our men got drunk. I took enough to strengthen and refresh, but not to inebriate, and traveled on. I got one of the artillery horses to ride and rode more than half way to camp, which we reached late in the evening. Camp was made tonight in the plaza of a small Mexican town where we got wood.[65] News reached us this morning that the yankees had started up the canion on the same road we took from Judge Baird's, and as soon as we heard it, Genl. Sibley hurried on to Albikirque as fast as possible. We came 18 miles today. The country is similar to the country below Albiquerque upon

---

65. Peticolas probably camped at the village of Alameda.

the river: wide valleys shut in by a range of mountains on each side and irrigated as below. I got to camp early and went into a Mexican ranch to warm my feet. The Mexican family were very civil and sat me a box to the fire.

Friday, 11 April 1862
We traveled through a continuous town this morning 7 miles till we reached Alberkerque, where we at last arrived perfectly worn out with our efforts. The main plaza of this town is quite neat, and a tall flag staff supports the Confederate flag, visible for miles. The Cathedral is a handsomer building than the one at Santa Fe and is the most conspicuous building in the city. We laid over the remainder of the day in a *Corrall* in front of the building in which Hardeman's forces are quartered. We saw all the boys that came back from San Antonio and they gave us a detailed account of the skirmishing of Canby's forces in front of the city.[66] I cannot say certainly that Canby only meant a feint upon the city to draw our forces down so that he might find a safe road to Ft Union, for the pickets of our forces heard him one night making a speech to them in which he begged them to charge the city and dig down the adobie walls if necessary, but I think that he had a twofold motive in this act: to take the city if possible while its defenders were reduced to the small number of 200, or failing in that, to make good his retreat to Union before we could countermarch upon him. He knew, too, that the 1500 we fought at Glorietta were still on the Pecos and that by affecting a junction with them he would be strong enough to meet us should we pursue him. The boys told us that the fighting was done almost entirely with Artillery. Canby had his two 24-pounders up and threw two or three bombs into the town, but did no damage. Our Artillery killed two or three of their men and wounded one who is now in town, a field officer, Major [Thomas] Duncan is his name I believe. Col. [Benjamin S.] Roberts is also reported by the Mexicans as killed. The *Abs* never came nearer than 800 yards to where our men with leveled guns awaited them behind Adobie walls. All of them unite in saying that if Green had gotten to Alberquerque a day sooner, they would have taken the whole outfit prisoners and had the artillery. They declare that there were only 400 or 500 regulars, and that the others were Mexicans, and that all of them were as

66. These were men of Capt. William P. Hardeman's Company A, the only First Regiment unit that did not participate in the Battle of Glorieta.

Peticolas sketches copied from those of a companion: A. "Church, Bona Lias [Bernalillo]." B. San Felipe de Neri Church, Albuquerque, with Confederate flag flying and mountain howitzers parked in plaza. The same cannons were later buried nearby. C. "1st Regt. Crossing River below Alberkirque, Apl 12th 1862." Peticolas is shown sketching the Fourth Texas Mounted Volunteer Regiment as it evacuated Albuquerque. (Arizona Historical Society)

cowardly as they could be. We hear, too, that there is not 10 days' rations for the Brigade above Craig, and that a march for the lower country is absolutely necessary to prevent our starving.[67] And here comes back the bitter regret that Sibley acted so recklessly as he did after the battle of Val Verde in not sending a force of 5 or 600 men on the best horses straight on to this place to prevent the enemy from destroying everything. Had this been done we would have had now two or 3 months' provisions for the whole brigade, for at least that much was destroyed here by the *Abs*, who hurried up directly after the battle for the express purpose of destroying it.

Saturday, 12 April 1862

Went down the river 3 miles this morning and began to make the crossing in a flatboat, which will take all day to cross the wagons. As I expected, night has come and all the company wagons of the first regiment have not crossed. Hardeman's wagons are still on the other side of the river.[68]

Sunday, 13 April 1862

We took up the line of march early this morning and traveled about 13 miles. We saw Judge Baird's ranch today and went through two mexican towns and one indian village near which we camped.[69]

---

67. The Texans were indeed in a bad position. A superior Union force was obviously uniting in the mountains to the east and would soon march against them. According to Sgt. James F. Starr, assigned to the adjutant general's office in Albuquerque, there was not enough ammunition left for a full day's fight, and rations for only twenty days remained. Sibley obviously had to leave for the Mesilla Valley, where Col. William Steele, Third Regiment, could provide some supply relief, but the lack of transportation hampered even that move. As a result, each company was allowed only one wagon, drawn by mules that were poor and weak. Unnecessary artillery was also left behind, with an unspecified number of cannons being buried in Santa Fe and eight of the ineffective mountain howitzers being similarly buried near the Albuquerque plaza to keep them out of Federal hands. These howitzers were located by Major Teel twenty-seven years later, in 1889, and subsequently unearthed. Two of the tubes are presently in the collection of the Albuquerque Museum. (Starr Campaign Letters, p. 179; Howard Bryan, "The Man Who Buried the Cannons," *New Mexico Magazine* 40 [January 1962]: 15.)

68. The crossing was near the village of Atrisco, now a part of Albuquerque's South Valley. Peticolas's camp was apparently near the crossing, on the west side of the Rio Grande.

69. The two towns were Pajarito and Los Padillas, and the First Regiment camp was near the Isleta Pueblo. That entire regiment, as well as the companies of the Third Regiment and Pyron's battalion, traveled southward along the Camino Real on the west side of the Rio Grande, while Colonel Green chose to follow a parallel

We are passing down on the right hand side of the river going down, and not on the same side we went up on. A train of wagons and the 2nd regiment are going down on the other side of the river. We have heard nothing of the yankees since we heard that they had reached Gallisteo going up. I think that they will go to Union. We are expecting, however, to have a fight down at Craig, which we are going down to take. Rumors reached us that Kit Carson and his regiment are there to hold the fort, but cannot tell certainly anything about it.

Monday, 14 April 1862

Traveled 10 or 12 miles today and camped in a little town where there is a large storehouse, the goods in which have been confiscated. The advance guard had a sharp skirmish at this place with a mexican company of the enemy and took one prisoner and two horses. The rest retreated rapidly towards Craig. We made a slow march today, for the road is very heavy with sand and our wagons cannot travel very fast. News reaches us that the *Abs* are following us closely. We saw a party on the other side of the river, of the enemy, this evening. Green, who had been coming down the river, was ordered to cross the river tonight; he did not do it, however.[70]

---

road on the east side of the river. Several Southern sympathizers, including Judge Baird and the merchants Rafael and Manuel Armijo, with their families, accompanied or followed Green's troops out of Albuquerque. (*O.R.* IX: 510–11; Giesecke Diary, entry for 13 April 1862.)

70. This camp was in the village of Los Lunas, some twenty-two miles south of Albuquerque. The enemy Peticolas mentions were undoubtedly Canby's scouts, who had watched Green's movement along the river. By the evening of 14 April, the Union commander knew the exact location of the Second Regiment's camp, which was in and around Governor Connelly's large residence and surrounding yards and fields, immediately north of the village of Peralta and about three miles from Sibley's main camp at Los Lunas. Normally a most excellent and vigilant officer, Colonel Green was careless this evening and neglected even to post outlying pickets. While the Texans moved southward, so did Canby. Leaving their camp in the Sandia Mountains early in the morning of 14 April, his Federal troops undertook a thirty-six-mile forced march through Tijeras Canyon, across present-day Kirtland Air Force Base and the Isleta Indian Reservation, striking the Rio Grande near Peralta about three o'clock in the morning of 15 April. The scene that greeted them was literally "music to their ears." The Texan officers were holding a raucous party in the governor's mansion as the enlisted men slept nearby. Maintaining silence, Canby positioned his infantry and battery of twenty-four-pounder howitzers north of the Rebels' camp, with the cavalrymen and McRae's light battery to the east. Some Union soldiers used the remaining hours of darkness to catch up on much-needed sleep, while others watched the Texans and anxiously awaited the upcoming fight. Lieutenant Bell, commanding McRae's Battery, observed:

Tuesday, 15 April 1862

We heard this morning that two of our men were killed last night sometime, or this morning, by the citizens of the mexican town we passed through just back of the indian town where our last camp was, and a company was sent back to demolish the town.[71] Later the Brigands came in with 25 mexican prisoners and said that they had come in on the company that killed our boys, killed two, and taken 25 prisoners; that they were not the citizens, but a company of Kit Carson's regiment.

We started early this morning but had hardly gotten under way when an express reached us that Col. Green had been attacked on the other side of the river; and we were countermarched, the wagons rapidly gotten together at our late place of encampment and corralled, and as ill luck would have it, Co. C was ordered to remain as wagon guard, [Lt. Ludwig von] Roeder being full Commander of the whole wagon guard and [Lt. Ferdinand K.] Fenner as acting adjutant. Being with the wagons, the boys asked me to take command of the company and keep them together. We had hardly gotten together and found out our full force under command of Major Teel before an express came to us that the enemy had sent a party around through the mountains to fall upon our trains and burn and destroy them. Captain [James] Walker assumed command, Roeder of our part of the forces, and I took charge of Co. C and got them all together. Then Genl. Sibley and Major Teel started off for the battle field 3 miles distant. I put mounted pickets out all around the town [of Los Lunas], and then, all formed in line, we waited with feverish anxiety for news from the battlefield. The first express that reached us was that Green had been surprised and knew nothing of the approach of the enemy till they began to fire into the camp; that he was camped in a very strong position with a wall and ditch on three sides, and that the *Abs* had taken and burnt 6 of our provision wagons and taken 15 prisoners.[72] Then the lookouts on the house tops dis-

---

The sounds of the fandango carried into the morning hours . . . [along with] the hilarious shout of some over-excited participant. All was merry as a feast within the dark outline of the town, just growing visible in the gloomy light of approaching day. There we lay in the restrained excitement of the situation. . . . (*O.R.* IX: 551, 665; Bell, "The Campaign of New Mexico," pp. 67–68.)

71. This bushwhacking attack against a small party of Second Regiment men was near Los Padillas. (Capt. J. B. McCown, Co. G, Fifth Texas, to editor, *Countryman*, 6 May 1862, in *The Bellville Countryman* [Texas], 7 June 1862.)

72. This early news from the Battle of Peralta was reasonably accurate. At dawn,

covered about 100 Cavalry up towards the mountain and in a moment every one was on the *qui vive*. A party of mounted men under Capt. [Henry E.] Loebnitz was sent out to skirmish with them, and we were stationed so as to defend every approach to our camp. The little howitzers, 4 in number, were placed so as to sweep every street and opening. Slow matches were lit and the guns heavily charged with canister.[73] Men from our company and other companies volunteered to man them. [Fridolin] Roth, [Samuel R.] Hyatt, [John M.] Owens, Coon [S. S. or Thomas M.] Field, and others were at one battery of 2 pieces, and strangers that I did not know were at the other pieces. Capt. Walker ordered me to hold the company in reserve till ordered to move, and at last he gave me command to hold a certain position behind an adobie wall that crosses the front of what was expected to be the line of battle. So off we went and took position as commanded, and remained there about 3/4 of an hour. While here we observed our skirmishers about 1200 yards off upon the confines of a little ranch towards the mountains; saw them maneuvering around, but as yet could not see the enemy. Presently our skirmishers came riding back and we found that the party we had been watching, supposed to be the enemy, were the brigands—our Santa Fe Company. We were then ordered back to the front of the house, and General Sibley, who had returned to us, put our men to work building a breastwork across in an oblique direction from the

---

Canby's artillery opened on Green's position, and the Confederate cannons replied in an ineffective exchange of solid shot and shell. However, the Union troops soon saw seven supply wagons, escorted by a mountain howitzer and one company of the Second Regiment, approaching Connelly's residence from the direction of Albuquerque. A mounted company of Colorado Volunteers charged this column, capturing the wagons, cannon, and twenty-two men, while four Texans were killed and six more wounded. One Union participant was mortally wounded. (*O.R.* IX: 551; Hollister, *Boldly They Rode*, pp. 92–93.)

73. Slow match was a type of punk, or slow-burning rope material, used to ignite the fuse that protruded into the powder chamber of cannons. By the time of the Civil War, however, a safer, more reliable system was in universal use. A friction primer was inserted into the touchhole that led to the powder chamber. When activated by the gunner, the primer's fulminate of mercury flashed through the touchhole, igniting the main powder charge and firing the cannon. Both sides used such tape-activated primers during the New Mexico campaign, as indicated by the editor's discovery of the primers at several artillery locations on the Glorieta battlefield. Use of the slow match indicated that the Texans were indeed very short of the essential supplies with which to fight. One Colorado Volunteer also supported this contention by observing that the Confederates had only the ineffective solid shot, rather than explosive shell and case shot, to fire at the Union positions. That factor probably contributed significantly to the low casualty rate at Peralta. (Ickis Diary, entry for 15 April 1862.)

The Church in Peralta, N.M., near the site of the battle of 15 April 1862. Copied by Peticolas from another soldier's drawing. (Arizona Historical Society)

corner of the large house to the corner of a smaller adobie building facing the river.

Meantime another express came from the field. Green had charged them, taken 17 wagons and a 24-pounder, and chased them three miles; that Scurry had crossed the river in the face of the enemy and under a heavy cannonading; that the 2nd regiment had been very anxious to have the Glorieta boys with them. Major Teel, Genl. Sibley, Capt. [Willis L.] Robards, and [Capt.] Loebnitz, when they went out to reach the battlefield, were cut off by a body of pickets who were stationed between us and the battlefield. They fired upon them several times and they were compelled to return. We had gotten our breast work of logs and a ditch finished, and had nearly all of us taken a recumbent position upon the plaza of the house to try to sleep, as the wind was blowing clouds of dust through the town and obscuring the view in every direction. But no express from the battlefield came to us for two long hours and through we would occasionally see a bomb burst afar off across the river. Oh the suspense of those two long hours! Who can tell how many a fearful and bloody tragedy was being inacted? How imminent was the peril in which we were all placed? Opposed to an enemy reported as 4000, we had only parts of the 3rd and Baylor's regiments, and the 1st and 2nd regiments, considerably weakened by pneumonia and two severe battles. Would fortune favor our arms and another victory be added to our list, or were we to be defeated and taken prisoners? All depended upon the fortune of the day. I never want to suffer as I did with anxiety that day again. At last, express came in that it was all over; the firing had ceased, but both parties were watching each other. And now we learned the truth of the whole transaction of the day. The whole action had consisted in the firing of a few shots with small arms and a few rounds of artillery from each side. Only one man was wounded on our side and he was accidentally shot by one of our own men. The enemy had an unknown quantity both killed and wounded—or in other words we know nothing about their loss. A prisoner, however, said that they had two or three hurt. They fell back after reconnoitering our position, though they had our men nearly surrounded, being unwilling to make the attack, and as they took a strong position and outnumber us so greatly, we did not venture to attack them.[74] They did burn 7 of our wagons, but all the rest of the news was bogus. It is almost impossible, in a country intersected with ditches and fences with adobie walls running in every direction, as in the Valley of the Rio Grande, to attack an army when it will not find upon some of its line an entrenchment and breastwork forming as secure a defense as though built under the special direction of a skillful engineer; and if the attacked party has any choice of position, it can always secure a very strong one.

---

74. While Green concentrated his men in a strong position behind the ditches and adobe walls that ran through the Connelly fields, Canby maintained a steady, though almost harmless, fire from his battery and infantrymen east of the Texans. He also sent a column of troops under Colonels Chivington and Paul around to the north and west of Connelly's residence. In accordance with his plan to force the Texans to retreat out of New Mexico rather than to fight and capture them, Canby forbade this encircling column to attack Green. They were, instead, to force Green's retreat from Peralta and to prevent his reinforcement from Sibley's main force west of the Rio Grande. Sibley and Scurry led the First Regiment, less Peticolas and Company C, across the icy river to Green's relief, but were repulsed by these Federals. In the meantime, a furious dust storm blew into the area, under the cover of which Green and Scurry withdrew the First and Second regiments during the late afternoon and night. One of the least bloody combats on record, the Battle of Peralta cost the Federals approximately four killed and three wounded (later reports being somewhat contradictory). Sibley reported only two more men wounded in addition to the losses sustained in the early capture of the wagon train. For a more detailed description of this fight, see Don E. Alberts, "The Battle of Peralta," *New Mexico Historical Review* 58 (October 1983): 369–79. (*O.R.* IX: 510, 551; Bell, "The Campaign of New Mexico," pp. 69–70; Hollister, *Boldly They Rode*, pp. 93–96; Howell Journal, entry for 15 April 1862.)

Green crossed his train this evening and tonight, and both regiments got to camp tired out, 1st with wet feet and tired limbs, about an hour before day.

Wednesday, 16 April 1862

We moved on today as soon as the brigade could be got under way. 1st and 3rd Regts. advance guard; the 2nd and Baylor's in the rear. They were put there doubtless because they were mounted. 2 or three companies of Cavalry have been dogging us down the river all day, trying to pick up stragglers, but cautious to keep out of range of our longest-range guns, and the whole command of the enemy, reported this morning to be camped about 5 miles behind us on the other side of the river, is moving down. We traveled about 15 miles, passed two of the camps we made going up, and came to halt at a little mexican ranch where we got plenty of wood.[75] The dust and sand has been extremely distressing all day as it blows over us in clouds and almost blinds us as we struggle along through the heavy sand. I neglected to state that by order of the General, we burnt and destroyed everything we had this morning save blankets, cooking utensils, a suit of clothes, and overcoats. This was to lighten our teams so that we could travel more rapidly. We rest well these nights after taking such long walks.

Thursday, 17 April 1862

We discovered that confounded cavalry of the enemy right opposite to us on the other side of the river this morning, and later we found that the whole force of the enemy had gained on us during the night and with all their wagons were moving steadily down the river on the other side just opposite to us. Our pickets and the enemy's advance of cavalry skirmished at intervals during the day across the river, but the enemy would never take up the gauntlet thus thrown down, but always retired to the hills. We looked for an attack today all day, but did not have our expectations realized, and it began to puzzle me to know what they were up to. The novel spectacle was here exposed of two hostile armies marching side by side down on opposite sides of the same river and in full view of each other. I watched with interest the long lines of Cavalry and infantry as they moved along their road, which is on the side of the

---

75. Their camp was near the town of Belen, where Peticolas had camped on 3 March 1862.

hill, and later in the evening when we had camped, I looked at them through a glass and saw them going into camp. I judged them to be between 2000 and 2500 men and a splendid train of about 100 wagons. They were evidently afraid of us and did not care to hazard crossing the river. I thought as I watched them that their idea was to beat us to Craig, throw heavy reinforcements into that fort enough to hold it, and then close in behind us and compel us to surrender. But I was sanguine of a different result. I judged the army opposite us to be the Pikes Peakers we fought at Glorieta and the 1200 with which Canby had attacked [defended] Craig, making in all about 2200 men. We know that Carson has 600 mexicans at Craig, but we despise rather than dread them, and these forces opposite us we have whipped some of them twice, and we are all confident that we can clean them up again. We are about 15 or 1800 strong, and think that we can get through to our supplies in the lower country.

We heard that our boys at Socoro had all been paroled by Canby, wounded and all, to prevent them from starving. They got out of provisions and Sibley sent them none from Alberkerque, so they had to surrender prisoners of war to get something to eat.

We traveled in all about 15 miles today and crossed a stream of water and camped on the far side, in full view of the enemy and out on the open prairie, and here it was we spied at the yankees.[76] We were here ordered to prepare as much provisions as we could and to prepare to travel tonight. One of our spies came in from behind this evening, from the top of the mountains behind us, and brings quite unpleasant news. He says that the main body of the enemy is not opposite us, but about 12 miles behind, where they are in great numbers. He says the front enemy is 3000 and the rear one 12,000, with an enormous train of wagons. Allowing something for an excited calculation, I judge them to be 6000 strong or there abouts, and now a good many of our apparently inexplicably rapid moves appear plain to me. Our leaders knew in Santa Fe that heavy reinforcements had arrived at Union; in fact, they got there a few days after the battle of Glorieta, as well as I can learn, and this is why we have been moving so rapidly. And now our position begins to be quite critical, and the object of the enemy begins to be apparent. They intend to surround us and hem us in on every side and

---

76. This camp was on the south bank of the Rio Puerco, near the present Interstate 25 bridge over that stream. The site was located in 1981 by Dee Brecheisen of Bosque Farms, New Mexico.

compel us to surrender, and we are in a fix: 6000 in the rear, 2000 on our flank, and 600 in a strong fort in front, and but one way to get out—without trains, wagons, artillery, etc. But we'll wait and see what tonight will bring forth. We are ordered to cook; we have cooked and packed mules with 10 days' rations and our blankets and a frying pan and coffee pot.

About 7 o'clock we started with our whole force, artillery and packs and a few wagons, to try Coopwood's route through the mountains to the lower country.[77] And now commenced one of the most remarkable retreats ever read of. We left all our most valued articles scattered over the ground in profusion; left the wagons and left our sick men huddled around a fire, with the yellow flag of our hospital waving over them from the corner of the wagon. It was affecting to see the brave companions in arms of these sick men grasping them by the hand and bidding them an affectionate farewell. "Good bye," said one as he squeezed his companion's hand, "The *abs* will take me in tomorrow morning." After some trouble we all got fairly started and marched till two o'clock up a gradual slope over rough uneven ground and then down a canion till we reached the hilly cedar country of the mountains.[78] We then halted and built large fires, spread our blankets around the blazes, and tired and sleepy after our 14-mile march, fell asleep and slept till

Friday, 18 April 1862

when we were aroused by Col. Scurry informing us that we would get breakfast 4 miles ahead where there was water. So we packed up our mules, swallowed a bite of bread, and started once

---

77. Two weeks earlier, Capt. Bethel Coopwood, San Elizario Spy Company, and a small party had come north to Albuquerque from the Mesilla Valley. To bypass Fort Craig, they had taken a series of remote trails along the eastern base of the San Mateo Mountains, west of the fort. Guided by natives familiar with the region's few water holes, the Texans then continued northward to the Rio Salado and thence to the Rio Grande at about the point where the Sibley Brigade was now camped. On the basis of that experience, and aided by a party of native New Mexicans known as "Aragon's men," Coopwood became the guide for the subsequent retreat southward around Fort Craig. (Starr Campaign Letters, p. 181; Julian J. Trujillo, Socorro, New Mexico, to C. A. Deane, Denver, Colorado, 9 May 1898, in Archives, Colorado Historical Association, Denver. This material was located and generously shared with the editor by William Elswick and Charles Counts of Denver.)

78. A modern, but poorly maintained, road across the La Jolla Game Preserve traces the Confederate route west-southwest from the Rio Puerco camp toward the south slopes of Ladron Peak.

more down the sandy Canion. The 4 miles proved to be about 8 before we walked it, and a good many of us were nearly broken down before we made the stop. We then came to salt water sink and camped for the remainder of the day, waiting for the 2nd Regt. Green, who started with about ½ his train, promises to leave it if we will wait for him. This water we found extremely unpalatable and salty, and the coffee made from it was hardly fit to drink atall, and as we had nothing but coffee and bread, we had pretty hard fare.[79]

Saturday, 19 April 1862

From our camp to the head of salt creek is 5 miles, from there to the next water (Bear Spring) 20, making in all 25 long miles that we traveled today. The brigade presents a singular appearance this morning. A great many of the infantry, tired of marching through the heavy sand, have picked up mules, little poor scrawny things, upon which they tie a fold of blankets for a saddle, and with a rope for a bridle strike out, every man for himself, upon the way. We have no road, and today the first mile or two was through a very narrow canion with perpendicular walls of rock on each side, and very boggy in the valley where the salt creek seeps, or crawls sluggishly along down the valley. We halted 15 or 20 minutes at the spring at the head of the creek and got a little bit to eat, and then struck out again up the long dusty sandy canion for 5 or 6 miles.[80] I had a mule that

---

79. Peticolas's camp was on the appropriately named Rio Salado near its junction with Silver Creek. The site was first identified through artifact evidence by Dee Brecheisen in 1979. He generously shared that information with the editor, who, with Dr. Philip Mead of Albuquerque, and Charles Counts and William Elswick of Denver, identified additional camp sites.

80. This spring, on the Ligon Ranch near the junction of the Rio Salado and La Jencia Creek, is known as Saracino Spring. After stopping briefly, Peticolas continued southward up the La Jencia bottom, then climbed out onto a large, flat plain bounded on the west and south by the Bear Mountains, north of present-day Magdalena, New Mexico. To further lighten their load, the Second Regiment, following Peticolas in the column, burned or otherwise destroyed in the Rio Salado canyon most of their remaining wheeled vehicles, along with excess artillery ammunition, and possibly three howitzers. The editor has seen the spot on La Jencia Creek where one of these cannons, a twelve-pounder mountain howitzer, was supposedly unearthed about 1950. It is a likely site, and the tube, which is genuine, is still located in nearby Socorro, New Mexico. Although he could not remember the exact number twenty-five years after the event, Major Teel claimed to have buried some cannons "in the mountains west of Fort Craig." The artillery chief also remembered having abandoned his carriage in the Rio Salado bottom. In it, wrapped in oilcloth around a roof support, was a highly prized oil painting of Napoleon Bonaparte that Teel had obtained from

I picked up to ride today, with a blanket saddle and old bridle. When we got to the point where you must leave the canion, the hill was extremely steep and high. Scurry got down from his horse, called for volunteers to help the artillery up the hill, and took hold of the cannon rope himself. Men flocked to the piece and the whole 5 were soon drawn safely to the top of the hill. Green has the other battery.[81] Then away, away, southwest across a vast plain, the way picked by our pilot (Capt. Coopwood) led. Four or five miles from where we left salt creek canion, three Antelopes started up from the grass and ran at full speed up the line of the command to get past to strike further west. A hundred guns were discharged at them and they were all killed. One got around the head of the column but was shot down just when about to make his escape. A few miles further on we crossed a tremendous canion, 500 feet deep, and here the artillery had to be drawn up the hill again by the men.[82] Late in the evening we finished this crossing with cannon, wagons, and all, and then began by a long gradual ascent to gain the summit of a pass in a range of high mountains that run across the course we must take. About sundown the advance reached the summit of this pass and still the water was six miles off, the water for which our famished throats were longing. A bear was killed near here by some of the

---

"one of the finest homes in Albuquerque." Having forgotten to remove the painting, Teel gave the matter little further thought, but was astonished to see it displayed, twenty-five years later, in an El Paso newspaper office. The paper's editor, it seems, had seen it hanging in the San Miguel church in Socorro, where the clergymen and parishioners thought it was a portrait of Saint Michael, patron saint of the church. He obtained the painting after convincing those in charge that its subject was no saint. (*O.R.* IX: 671–72; Howell Journal, entry for 19 April 1862; Bryan, "The Man Who Buried the Cannons," 15, 35.)

81. General Sibley appears to have displayed little or no leadership during the entire Confederate retreat, with Colonel Green and Lieutenant Colonel Scurry making most of the practical decisions. These commanders, especially Scurry, were determined to bring the captured guns of McRae's Battery back to Texas as the only tangible trophies of their otherwise disastrous campaign. Whether the six original cannons were still together, or whether only five had been retained and were in the care of the First Regiment, cannot be positively determined. At the time, individual artillery pieces assigned to posts and units were not listed by serial numbers, so a rigorous accounting of the guns used by the Union and Confederate forces in New Mexico is not possible. However, regardless of which regiment had which cannons, the Texans brought nine pieces through safely to the Mesilla Valley and subsequently into Franklin and Fort Bliss. (Starr Campaign Letters, p. 181.)

82. This obstacle was the upper canyon of La Jencia Creek, which had turned westward after the Texans left it earlier and now again lay across their route. It is not 500 feet deep, nor very steep-sided, but undoubtedly seemed so to weary, thirsty soldiers at dusk.

men, that would weigh 400 lbs. And now pines were plentiful all along the road. No order was observed, no company staid together, the wearied sank down upon the grass, regardless of the cold, to rest and sleep; the strong, with words of execration upon their lips, pressed feverishly and frantically on for water. Dozens fell in together and in despair gave up all hope of getting to water and stopped, built fires and fell asleep. Packs slipped off the bare-backed mules, and mules gave out and refused to move further, and on, on struggled the main column, through scenery the grandest and most picturesque imaginable. We have quite a number of women along, the wives and daughters of Mexican citizens who have thought it most prudent for them to leave because of their southern principles, and these people have light wagons and ambulances along, to take their provisions and property along.[83]

And now the cry became more intense and universal for water, water. At every fire we stopped to inquire the distance to water. Every fire or cluster of fires on ahead was the main camp where water and rest were to be had, and every hope of this sort was blasted when we came up to them. We began now to get deep down in the valley, where larger pine trees flourished, and the woods began to be dense and timber heavy. At last we reached the main camp where the whole brigade was to camp, where members of the advance had camped without regard to order of regiments or companies.[84] For

---

83. The spectacle of these civilians riding in relative comfort while the soldiers struggled along on foot infuriated many of the men, especially those suffering from pneumonia and measles. Private W. R. Howell of the Second Regiment observed that, "My health is very bad, yet I am compelled to walk while mean Mexican women ride." (Howell Journal, entry for 21 April 1862.)

84. Peticolas's camp was at a large spring, Ojo del Pueblo, located about one mile northwest of present-day Magdalena, New Mexico, and named for the nearby ruins of an old Indian village. A month later, Capt. James "Paddy" Graydon, commanding Canby's "spy company," retraced the retreat route in reverse and reported that at Ojo del Pueblo the Texans "blew up a caisson, burned three wagons, hospital department, medicines, etc.; left a few shell and round shot." He described the road Peticolas had just traveled as being "strewn with old harness, iron ovens, and in fact everything but small [arms] ammunition." It is possible that men of other units camped at different water holes. Several journals mention Bear Springs, and indeed, a spring by that name is located seven miles north of Ojo del Pueblo. However, neither the topography nor distance to Bear Springs matches Peticolas's description, and his distance estimates were generally very accurate. The use of the term may have come from the bear story related by several of the men. Some soldiers may also have continued eight miles farther to Texas Spring, although there is no artifact evidence to indicate that such was the case. (O.R. IX: 571–72; Starr Campaign Letters, p. 181; Giesecke Diary, entry for 19 April 1862.)

hours as the scattered men came in, a confusion of voices hallooing for different companies, individuals, and regiments rendered the place a perfect babel. I was leading our packhorse and lost blankets, overcoats, and everything that was under the pack. After a long time I found our mess, and seizing a full canteen of water, I laid back and drank, forgetful of everything and everybody around me.

Three bears were found by the advance at the spring, but they made their escape. We supped heartily of bread and coffee, our only diet now, and fell asleep. The supply of water is plentiful here, but it was all soon muddied up by the rush of horses into the spring. We had several riding mules, and the blankets were fortunately saved and were the property of different members of the mess, so that we succeeded in having blankets for a light bed for each.

Sunday, 20 April 1862

Some talk of spiking the artillery and leaving it; 2nd Regt. and Green have gotten tired in one day of helping their battery along, but it was not done. Scurry undertakes to take them through and will not consent to leave behind us the only trophies we have been able to keep of our victories. With his command he expects to take them through a wild, broken, mountainous country for 90 miles where never wheel ran before. He has command now of Baylor's men, the fragment of the 3rd Regt., and the first Regt. We started about 9 A.M. this morning and traveled 15 miles over a rolling country to the next water. We commenced by climbing a mountain, descending into a valley, and then by a gradual ascent passing through a chain of hills, through a canion. From thence our road lay over a broad stretch of rolling country, destitute of timber but affording a pretty good road. We got to camp about ½ an hour by sun and got wood together and went to cooking. We found only water enough here to cook with and drink, but none for our mules and horses.[85]

Monday, 21 April 1862

On this day, marking the 2nd month since our *Val Verde* battle, we traveled 16 miles; down the valley in which we had found water and then across the mountains again, and passed in sight of Ft. Craig. Every man knew the *table* mountain and could distinguish

---

85. The route was generally that of present-day New Mexico Highway 107, along the western base of the Magdalena Mountains, but veering eastward to the skimpy water supply at Alameda Spring, near the southern end of that range.

the glistening waters of the river away down in the valley 10 miles from where we were crawling along the side of the mountain. We traveled along in full view of this rather (to us) noted place for two hours. Climbed a high steep hill, dragging up the 8 [9] heavy guns, and at last, late in the evening, struck camp in a narrow canion a mile from the water, but to which there was no nearer approach for any vehicle on wheels. We took our pack mules over the hill, almost too steep for any four-footed animal to go down, and stopped at the water at the bottom of the hill. We were now indeed in the Mountains; vast rocky peaks rise up so high as to make one giddy to look up at them. Towering pines shoot up from amongst the rocky cliffs and the little stream of water in the gully below is as cold as ice. We camped on a little flat close to the water, turned our horses out upon the hill, and got our supper.[86]

Tuesday, 22 April 1862

The weather is getting milder rapidly. We started early this morning and the companies each were given a cannon to take through. Scurry informed us that this was in order to enable us to go straight on without so many halts. He informed us that he had committed to us the guns and that we were to be responsible for their safe passage through. We have 9 guns. Co. C and D take one. We traveled some 5 or 6 miles, helping our gun up the worst hills, when we suddenly came on to a vast canion running directly across our direction and seemingly impassible.[87] Both banks were extremely high and steep, and there seemed no chance to cross. But nothing daunted, we locked the wheels and our guns were slided down the hill, with men holding back by a long rope. Then up the next hill

---

86. The Texan retreat continued southwestward across the narrow valley separating the Magdalena and San Mateo mountains, then along the lower slopes of the latter range, from where Fort Craig and Black Mesa are visible at a distance of approximately twenty-five miles. Following an old trail farther into the mountains, Sibley's men camped in an opening at the head of Horse Mountain Canyon, known today as the Park. From there, Peticolas and others took the animals a mile west to water in the bottom of East Red Canyon and camped there, about one-and-a-half miles above Turkey Springs. Although the editor and his wife have found some artifact evidence of this camp, its exact location and extent have not been determined.

87. This barrier was East Red Canyon near the point where it emerges from the mountains. The Texans had retraced the last two miles of their previous day's journey, then turned southward, traveling near the eastern base of the San Mateo Mountains. There were no very high hills to climb, but the route crossed the head of every one of the numerous parallel canyons that run eastward from the San Mateo range to the valley of the Rio Grande.

114

we dragged the pieces, "with many a weary step and many a groan." When we got to the top of this hill we were all exhausted, but on moved the Artillery, and on went we. "Company A's gun is stalled, by G——d," said Scurry when the first gun struck the foot of the hill and would not go up. Immediately the men sprang up to the ropes and the gun went up. We were now about all out of water. Our canteens were empty and we soon began to suffer for want of it. Water is still 10 miles ahead and the column is already reeking with sweat and parched with thirst in the warm spring sun. Up another Mountain and down and up and down and so we travel on. Late in the evening after sundown, the advance reached Alamosa Canion and found plenty of water.[88] About dark, J. I. Hughes and myself were weaving recklessly down the steep hill on the left of the canion containing the water. With lips black and parched, and throats swelled and dry, and breath hot and voice husky, we dashed recklessly down the steep sides of the rocky canion, jostled roughly against men who were climbing up satiated with water, dashed up loose stones from the hill that went thundering down to the bottom; and on we rushed till we reached the water and there we threw ourselves upon the rocks, regardless of the crowding horses and mules, regardless of the swearing men, regardless of everything, and drank the cool clear soft water; drank till we sank back completely satiated. Oh, the water, the good water!! Here we camped as we did last night, with no guard, and our artillery 1/2 a mile from the water.

Wednesday, 23 April 1862

We traveled 25 miles yesterday; today we traveled 18 or 20 over a better road than we have had. We have had only three very steep high Mountains to work our artillery over, and have been traveling slowly. About 5 o'clock P.M. we reached some holes of water and drank heartily. There was not enough water for the stock, and we did not stop all night, but started across the plain for the next water, said to be 4 1/2 miles from this water. We traveled 8 miles across that

---

88. Most of the Texans who kept journals on this retreat mistook the location of this camp. The water was actually the small stream issuing from Nogalita Spring, in Nogal Canyon, as indicated by excellent artifact evidence found in the vicinity. "Paddy" Graydon also identified the site during May 1862, and described some of the hardships endured by the Confederates as they struggled southward this day. "On the road," he reported, they "left three dead bodies half buried. In another place [we] found bones of a man's arm, half eaten by wolves. I had all buried." (O.R. IX: 671–72.)

plain till late at night and found no water, and so we made a dry camp with nothing to eat or drink, and slept all night.[89]

Thursday, 24 April 1862

Early this morning, with bodies unrefreshed and both hungry and thirsty, we made a start for the water that Coopwood had found during the night, which was reported 4 miles off. We reached it about 9 o'clock and found it to be a small rapid stream of water in the valley of an immense canion, 800 or 1000 feet deep.[90] We made the descent of the mountain with more ease than I expected, as we found a long canion running down into the valley that we went down. We went to work and cooked and ate heartily, as our long fast justified us in doing, but we had only bread and coffee, and have had that diet for 5 days. We laid over on this creek, which is called the Hondo, all day, and rested our worn-out artillery teams. In the evening we worked our cannons up the steep hill, a half a mile long, on the South side of the canion, and after supper we went up there with full canteens and camped.

There have been a long list of promotions in our brigade in these two months that I have neglected to notice in their proper order. 1st, after Glorieta battle, Scurry was made Colonel and Pyron Lieut. Col. of a new Regiment to be raised for this brigade. After the successful defense of Alberkurque, and because he was Senior Capt. and entitled to it, Hardeman was promoted to the rank of Lieut. Col. of the 1st. Regt. [Andrew J.] Scarborough, Capt. of Co. B, having acted cowardly at *Glorieta*, was passed over, and [George J.] Hampton, Capt. of Co. C, appointed major, leaving this company without a captain, which we have to elect when our whole company gets together again. [Lt.] Charles Linn, Arch [J.] McNeill, and Jas. [Cpl. James J.] Hall of our company got to us tonight from Steele's Command and a good many others of other Companies and regiments. Col. Reily also got [in], and they brought our mail up so that there

---

89. Peticolas had passed Peñasco Spring, then continued southward approximately six miles over the plain north of Monticello Canyon, to camp three miles short of water.

90. Here at last was the long-awaited Alamosa River, in the bottom of Monticello Canyon, about two miles west of present-day Interstate 25. Some Texans referred to the stream as the Amilla, while Peticolas believed it to be the Hondo, perhaps indicating that in the later stages of the retreat, Coopwood's native guides, who could have recognized such a well-known landmark, had deserted or been dismissed.

was great jubilee in camp over news from home.[91] Messes sat up late reading letters and discussing their contents and talking with the *green* men who had come in, and there was a great and general stir in camp which did not calm down till 10 o'clock that night.

Friday, 25 April 1862

We crossed the *mesa* today to the first water hole in the famous *Sheep Canion* that we (Co's C and G) traveled up about 3 months ago under Major Raguet after indians. The Cotton woods were green and the weedy undergrowth of the Canion green, and everything betokens the incoming Spring. We found Col. Steele's fires still burning, but his command had moved on to the river and we followed him. Twas 5 miles to the Canion and 12 to the river from the water down the canion, so when we reached the valley of the Rio Grande once more we struck camps and staid all night.[92]

Saturday, 26 April 1862

We wrote letters yesterday evening that Scurry said he would take home for us. He gave up commanding the regiment yesterday to Col. Reily. Made an affecting farewell speech to the men, which unfortunately I did not hear, in which he referred to our victories, our trials, and our privations, and said that it was like taking leave of wife and children to take leave of us who had fought with him so bravely and been with him so long. He shed tears as he bade the men farewell. Thus we lost the best officer, most polished gentleman, most sociable gentleman, and the most popular Col. in the whole outfit. Coopwood has been appointed Major of the new regiment to be raised, and Adjutant [Ellsberry R.] Lane is going back to be Scurry's Adjutant. Coopwood is a brave man, a good fighter, and deserves promotion for successfully guiding the brigade through the

---

91. At this time, Colonel Reily assumed command of the First Regiment from Scurry, who had led it in battle as lieutenant colonel. Scurry had been promoted to colonel of the new, undesignated regiment as of 21 February 1862, for "gallant and meritorious conduct in the battle of Valverde." (Hall, *Confederate Army of New Mexico*, p. 56.)

92. The route on this final day of the Texans' "mountain detour" lay due south across the flat plain between Monticello Canyon and Cuchillo Negro Creek. Following the latter stream to its junction with the Rio Grande and the main river road, Peticolas camped just north of the present town of Truth or Consequences, New Mexico, some forty miles south of Fort Craig. His notable journey had covered approximately one hundred miles and taken eight days.

mountains around Craig. Volney Rose, Jesse Wheeler, and John Waf-
ford go back with Scurry as escort. They would hardly be missed,
as they were all in the Commissary department and hardly even in
the Company. Adjutant Lane took leave of us this morning, hoping
that we would have a good Adjutant. We traveled 17 miles and
camped about 1 mile below Coopwood's battle ground.[93] Rations
all out tonight.

Sunday, 27 April 1862

Today we made a *short* journey of about 20 miles to meet the
provision train Steele had started up to us. We ate for breakfast this
morning a rib or two of an old broke-down work ox we had along,
without salt. Yesterday two men were left on the road, too sick to
be moved. We also left two in the mountains near Craig. They were
thrown out of the wagons by Major [Richard T.] Brownrigg and one
out of [the] end of Sibley's wagon. Sibley is heartily despised by
every man in the brigade for his want of feeling, poor generalship,
and cowardice. Several Mexican whores can find room to ride in his
wagons while the poor private soldier is thrown out to die on the
way. The feeling and expression of the whole brigade is never to
come up here again unless mounted and under a different general.[94]
We camped 7 miles above Ft. Thorn and found our provision train
there. We all ate heartily of bread and coffee, but got nothing else
brought us.

Monday, 28 April 1862

We made a short march today of 8 miles. Passed our old camp
above Thorn where we were lying when the sutler came up, and
camped in a cottonwood grove about a mile below the fort. Smallpox
begins to prevail to a considerable extent amongst the soldiers, and

---

93. This camp was near Seco Creek, beneath the present-day Caballo Reservoir.
The battleground to which Peticolas refers was the site of a skirmish between Coopwood's company and a patrol of regular cavalrymen from Fort Craig on 26 September
1861. (*O.R.* IV: 27–32.)

94. General Sibley found few defenders among the members of his brigade. Sgt.
James F. Starr, of the Second Regiment, observed in a letter to his father:

> Among the soldiers I hear ridicule and curses heaped upon the head
> of our genl. They call him a coward, which appears very plausible
> too, for he has never been in an engagement or where there was any
> appearance of there going to be one—Bad Management has been the
> cause of our ruin. . . ." (Starr Campaign Letters, p. 182.)

pneumonia also. Al Field, [Philip] Meyer, and [Hermann] Seidel got into camp tonight. They were left at Socoro. They confirm the news that we heard about that they were all prisoners, and inform us that they first took the hospital oath not to leave Socoro, to attempt to rejoin the command, or go anywhere under 30 days, nor then without giving Canby notice. Upon this they all got 10 days' rations. When Canby came down after Sibley's retiring brigade, after we had started round Craig through the mountains, Dr. [Edward N.] Covey surrendered the hospital and attendants into Canby's hands. He took them all down to the Fort Craig, where he paroled them and turned them loose to go to Messilla with 6 days' rations. When Al reached us, they had been 5 days on the road and were out of grub.

From Field I glean much interesting information. He says that Canby has acknowledged that if we had formed a line of battle the next morning after the battle of *Val Verde* before Craig, and demanded a surrender, that they should have had the fort without the fire of a gun. One of the 24-pound guns was dismounted and the other in the river, so that they could [not] have made successful resistance. Al says that from all he could learn, they had 6600 and some odd men on the field that day (21st Feby.), 1100 regulars and Regt. Colorado Volunteers, and the remainder mexicans; that 2¹/₂ Regiments ran off after the battle and never came back; that it was an error in us to suppose that Carson's men were one of these Regiments; that he has them yet. He also told me that all the men who were with Canby when he last came down were pikes peak men, Colorado Volunteers and Regulars, and no mexicans; that he had 3000 of them or thereabouts. The enemy claims to have whipped us in every battle and think we are sick of them. They make a good deal of sport of our retreat through the mountains round Craig. O'Graden's [Graydon's] Spy Co. knew every move we made, and O'Graden [Capt. James "Paddy" Graydon] himself was looking at us when we drilled at Ft. Davis coming on up. They boast that some of their spys took supper with us every night we were in New Mexico. O'Graden reported us at the Mountain Springs, camped one night when we were coming round Craig, and the whole Army being there, they started off in high spirits to cut us off from the river at Alamosa. The regulars didn't go, but all the rest did. The brass band was playing Yankee Doodle when they started off, the U.S. flag flying, the Pikes Peak union colors waving, and everything betokened an army confident of success. Al told one of them that if they met Sibley they would

Col. Christopher C. "Kit" Carson, commanding the First New Mexico Volunteer Regiment. (National Archives)

come back in little squads like a drove of sheep that had been scattered. They went out, camped 4 miles from the Ft., staid all night, and next day they went back.[95]

Kit Carson is a low, square-set, old plain farmer-looking man with a slow, quiet speech and a good deal of accommodation. Canby is 6-ft, 3-in high and large in proportion, weighing say (200 lbs.), with grey beard and hair, good countenance, and the habit of always keeping a cigar between his lips pendant, but never lit. He is very reserved and says but little. No man in his camp knows at night what he is going to do next morning. He has been promoted and is now Brigadier General. A Kentuckian by birth and a soldier by profession, his acts towards those of our men who have fallen into his hands have proved him to be a perfect gentleman.

Al says the Regimental flag of the Pikes Peak men is a blue ground and the eagle of america in the center bearing in its beak the motto "E Pluribus Unum." Al was all over Ft. Craig and says that it is by no means a strong place, that 6-lb. balls would shatter them [the walls] all to pieces. Dr. [Henry J.] Hunter has promised to draw a plan of the whole fort when we get down below. [Robert

95. There is no other mention in journals or official reports of such an expedition.

120

J.] O'Grady of Baylor's regiment, Sergt. Major, who was said to have deserted, gave himself up and was paroled. The sentinel who took him said that he could have gotten away if he had wished, as he [O'Grady] had a sharp shooter and six shooter, and he had nothing but a musket and bayonet, but he would not halt but rode right up to him till the bayonet struck his horse's throat. Supposition is that he was drunk or tired of the service. [E. J.] Cook, wounded in the thigh, came down to Craig, and Al thinks he has deserted us. Morris Lichtenstein and 30 others started up to join the command before they took the hospital oath, with a gun, six shooter, blanket, and 3 days' rations apiece. With the exception of 5 men who broke down and returned, nothing has ever been heard of them and no one knows what has become of them.

And now for some other items. Pikes Peak men know Scurry and dread him accordingly. They said that at Glorieta, Scurry, when wishing the men to charge Pigeon's Ranch, said "That ranch, boys; heaven or hell." And just here I must say a word about Pack Mules to explain subsequent events. Every morning there has been more or less trouble about pack mules. An indiscriminate course of appropriation has been adopted by the brigade (to call it by no harsher name). One mess will pack up and start off with the best mule they can get, without regard to who packed the mule the day before, or since we began our march round the mountains from above Socoro. Thus we have frequently had to pack different mules and often to wait till the regiment moved before we could get any mule atall. Today we had a poor broken-down mule, and if we had made a long march, the animal could never have made it. We had a first-rate pack mule when we first started from the river, but when we got to the hill where we came out of Salt Creek Canion, Hardeman went around getting all the best mules to hitch to the Artillery, and ours was unpacked and taken. He gave us in the place of our mule an old broken-down, sore-backed Artillery horse that only carried our provisions and grub one day and then gave out. So, on

Tuesday, 29 April 1862

when we had gotten through breakfast and were ordered to march, we did not find our pack mules, nor did we get any mule atall, though we waited till the whole brigade moved off. I went to Hardeman, Lieut. Col. Commanding, but he told me to wait and pick up a mule. I spoke to Lieut. Linn, Commanding, but he said he couldn't help us, and so we waited till all were gone and thought we would find some mule on the way, but we did not succeed and had the alternative presented to us to leave cooking utensils, coffee, meal, coats, and everything, pack them on our backs, or make a raft and come down the river. We concluded to try the latter; found some logs that had been used for building a house and that were dry and light, fastened them together with green raw-hide string to cross pieces, and in short made a pretty good little raft. It was at first thought to be wide enough to take us all and our baggage together, but when it was launched we found that it would just snugly bear up our baggage and two men, so the rest of us concluded to take it afoot, and Jas. Hughes and Ruben Purcell went on board and took charge of our baggage. We traveled 16 miles and crossed the river at the San Diego river [crossing]. The stream was up and the ford rapid and deep, but we did not much mind wading as the water is comparatively warm, the weather growing rapidly warmer every day. I was in washing yesterday and took off and kept off my flannel shirt. We slept tonight by a log set on fire, without any blankets or coats, and slept tolerably well. The raft did not get down tonight and we concluded that Rube and Jim had stopped and camped on the river somewhere, not caring to steer in the night. They were seen at a bend in the river six miles from the crossing, but the river makes several wide bends between this point and the crossing, and the distance must be 15 miles.

Wednesday, 30 April 1862

Last day of the month. No raft as yet. Our mess waited till 10 o'clock for it but it came not, and Davis and myself got two stray horses, mounted them, and started on to camp. We left the river and climbed the hills and passed over and down on the other side, and reached the river at Roblero [Robledo]. Camped two or three miles down the river in a grove of cottonwoods. We (i.e., our mess) have to borrow all cooking utensils and cups, etc., and we have a good deal of trouble to get anything to cook in and are living on bread and beef without salt. No rafts or raftsmen came tonight and we slept under one blanket, one that I found at camp this morning.

Thursday, 1 May 1862

Came about 10 miles today and camped between Donna Anna and Las Cruces. [A. S.] Woulfe and [Gustavus] Schraeder came in to the company today, and [Wiley J.] Whitley. We are beginning to get uneasy about Rube and Jas. They have not made their appearance yet. I rode my horse again today. He has a very sore back, but I roll the blankets in a heavy roll on each side and thus keep the saddle off the sore.

Friday, 2 May 1862

Traveled about 10 miles today and camped about noon 2½ miles below Ft. Fillmore. We passed through Las Cruces where the 2nd Regiment has stopped. As I understand it, the 3rd Regt. has received orders to remain in camp where it is till further orders. The 2nd Regt. stops at Las Cruces and Fillmore and we go to the cottonwoods and Bliss. We are slowly recruiting by traveling this easy journey, and every now and then some member of Company C can be heard humming a tune, some familiar air or favorite love song, but often the tune is stopped when memory brings back some remembrance of our hardships, and then the singer seems for a few minutes ashamed of his cheerfulness; but a better trend of feeling and more cheerfulness begins [to] characterize the Company and faces look less careworn and elongated. Rube and Jim Hughes came in this evening with 3 mules and all our luggage that they had on the raft. They were very tired and hungry, and we ministered to their wants, for we were rejoiced to see them, especially as they brought in our blankets. They had a pleasant trip for two days living on beef and coffee, without salt. They were under some apprehension from the indians and saw plenty of beavers and wolves and turkeys, but did not kill any of them as they did not want to waste their ammunition or discover their whereabouts to the Indians if any were about. They saw ½ a dozen suspicious-looking Mexicans, well armed, who said they were going to Donna Ana, but were not molested. At the end of the 2nd day's journey they got to the San Diego crossing of the river and where we camped the same night we left them. There they found 3 mules and packed the things upon them, moored the raft, and took it afoot with their mules across the hill and down the same road we traveled. They camped with the 3rd Regt. last night, and tonight are with us.

Saturday, 3 May 1862

We left the water holes this morning and marched past *Willow Bar* and on to the upper edge of *The Cottonwoods* where we lost our horses by (we thought the Indians, but O'Graden says by his) Mex-

"Infantry—Modern style of carrying a gun on the march."
Peticolas's sketch of one of his companions dressed mostly in
captured Federal uniform components and carrying a "minie-
gun." It is slung over his shoulder rather than across the back, as
was common. This is one of very few known sketches of actual
participants in the Sibley campaign, one other being Peticolas's
self-portrait drawn after the New Mexico campaign. (Peticolas
Journal)

icans. At Willow Bar we camped a good long time when we came up, and it was here we spent Christmas. We came in all some 15 or 18 miles and camped about noon.[96]

Sunday, 4 May 1862

We have lost nearly all memory of the day of rest. We have nothing when Sunday comes to remind us that it is Sunday. Numbers [of men] don't know the day of the week at all and don't much care to know it. If they keep the day of the month they esteem themselves lucky, and now nothing distinguishes the Sabbath from any other day. We traveled 18 miles today and camped 6 miles from Bliss. Learned yesterday that [C. B.] Callender and John A. Warburton are exchanged. Callender has started for home with Colonel Scurry, but we don't know yet how much further he has gotten than Ft. Bliss. If he is there he will not get to go home.

Monday, 5 May 1862

We climbed the hills over which the road runs at an early hour this morning and for the first time since we left Alymosa creek we are marching in order. Looking down upon the turbid waters of the Rio Grande rushing through this pass in a great chain of mountains that here crosses its way, seemingly to bar it up and stop it alltogether, we marched along the hills, passed Judge [Simeon] Hart's and at last reached Franklin, where Co. A had stopped. We heard a good deal of news from the old states when we reached this place. I read more particulars of the great battle on the edge of Tennessee near Corinth, Miss. in which our troops took the first day 100 cannon and all the baggage trains, ammunition, and camp equipage of the Federal army and the 2nd day took 18 more batteries and 5000 prisoners, driving the enemy across the river with great slaughter. 15,000 of the enemy killed and wounded, from 4 to 5000 of ours. Also of the death of Lieut. Gen'l. A. S. Johnston in this battle, and further that [Gen. P. G. T.] Beauregard is unhurt.[97] We are in quarters

---

96. Company C had camped at the Cottonwoods, some twenty-three miles from Fort Bliss, for about a week after Christmas 1861.

97. This was the Battle of Shiloh, fought on 6–7 April 1862, as Peticolas rested in Santa Fe. The first of the great battles in the western theater, Shiloh's casualty rates shocked the nation. The first day's fight was a triumph for the Confederates, but on the second day, Gen. Ulysses S. Grant's Federal army counterattacked, winning an impressive victory.

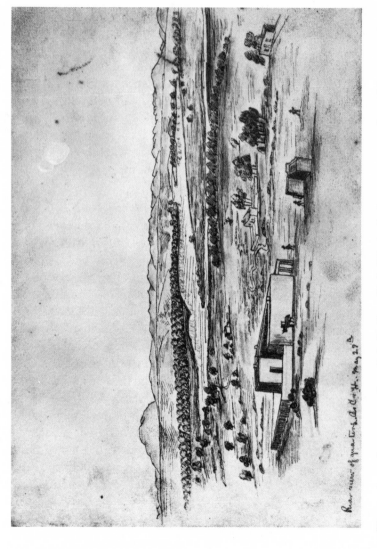

"Rear view of quarters. Cos. C & G, May 27th." Peticolas's quarters as the Sibley Brigade rested at Franklin, Texas, after the New Mexico campaign, looking south across the Rio Grande to site of present-day Ciudad Juarez. (Arizona Historical Society)

now in Franklin, the whole Company in one large room in a large adobe building, with a piazza in front and a court in the rear, but the work of getting clothes and cooking utensils for us goes on slowly.

Tuesday, 6 May 1862

Heard today that Canby had come down with a flag of truce and the order to Sibley to remove his sick and wounded from New Mexico as he had no provisions for them. He also brings news of an armistice of 90 days between the contending powers.[98]

Wednesday, 7 May 1862

In quarters today. Nothing unusual going on.

Thursday, 8 May 1862

Letter writing is all that we do today. Everybody is writing long letters home. Talk about an approaching election in our Company, for Captn., talked of. [Lieutenants] Linn and Fenner will be the only candidates, and from appearances, Fenner will be elected. Linn had to stay back at Thorn in charge of that post and did not go above with us into New Mexico. He has not had an opportunity, consequently, to show what soldierly qualities he possesses.

Friday, 9 May 1862

News reached us today that [Otto] Kleberg is *Missing*. He left the hospital at Donna Ana and has not been heard of since. This is the 2nd man of Co. C that has gone this way. Of all the accounts of the way in which soldiers go, set upon the face of the muster roll, this is the saddest, suggests the greatest variety of ideas, and is the most painful. If a man is dead, we know he is gone forever and the great secret of life is revealed to him; if he is wounded, the mind has something certain to dwell upon, but missing!! Where is he? What is he doing? What is his condition? Alas, tis all uncertainty. The wolves of the forest may be making their foul feasts from his bleeding frame; the fierce Indian may be wearing his scalp, a trophy of easy victory, at his girdle. Sick and faint, he may be lying on some solitary road, vainly calling for friends to help him. Perhaps sick and faint, burning with fever and consumed with thirst, he is groveling in the hot sand and praying to die. —Missing—!! For him no friendly hand prepares a soldier's grave; no gallant comrade in arms

---

98. These were both false rumors.

stoops over him to wrap the blanket about the still form and exclaim with a sigh, "A brave soldier lies here." No mother has a line from a messmate informing her how and where her son fell.

Saturday, 10 May 1862

We held our election today for Captain under an order from Col. Reily. [1st Lt.] Linn and [2d Lt.] Fenner were the only two candidates. 51 votes was the total cast. Of these, Linn received 24 and Fenner 27, Fenner being elected by the meager majority of 3 votes. Linn was my choice for Captain, as he has more command about him than Fenner, and the men respect him more. 3rd Lieutenancy being then vacant, an order from Col. Reily was immediately procured and the men told to nominate candidates for that office. [Cpl.] L. Bartlett, myself, and [Sgt.] Jas. Coffee were nominated. On the first ballot I received 23 votes, Bart 19, and Coffee 9. Coffee then withdrew from the race and Bart and I ran. I received 24, he 26, so he was elected by 2 majority. I was very much surprised to learn after the election that Frank Kreidler and John Kuykendall had both voted against me. I got all the German vote. I have concerned myself very little about the election and never asked a man in the Company to vote for me. Bart promised Kreidler to help him get a horse, and this bought his vote in the 2nd race. If this vote had not been thus bought, it would have been a tie. This evening [Fridolin] Roth, [Thomas M.] Clark, [William] Trautwein, [Julius] Jenke, and [Otto] Kleberg got here from above, and their chagrin can be easily imagined when they found the election over and two men that they did not want in office. Their votes would have changed the whole face of the election. Linn would have gotten 4 out of the 5 votes, which would have elected him by one vote, and I would also have gotten the same vote for Linn's place and thus would have been elected also by two votes. "Spilt milk."

Sunday, 11 May 1862

Lying in camp eating scant rations and wishing for a change of clothes. News comes from below that the long-looked-for train bringing up the clothing, etc., sent us from Victoria is near at hand. Ship up from Ft. Quitman brings this news. We wait impatiently. Most of us are wearing the same suit we started from Santa Fe in. Took a couple of sketches today and visited Ft. Bliss, where the shade trees are in full leaf.

Monday, 12 May 1862

Still lying in camp. Talk of a baker to bake bread for the Company. The Paymaster has been up a week and is busy paying off the troops. Coffee is making out a muster roll; a tedious job. Clark is quite sick. John Kuykendall and W. B. James are down with the measles. Major Hampton is dangerously sick and has been delirious. Lieut. Roeder has been unwell for several days and is now taking the measles. Clark and W. B. James have gone to the hospital. John Kuykendall refuses to go, though he has a contagious disease. Guard has been discontinued since Fenner's promotion. A good portion of the Company are highly dissatisfied with the officers click [*sic*] and talk of leaving the Company and joining the artillery Company being made up to take the guns we have.[99]

Tuesday, 13 May 1862

Reading "History of the French Revolution" as a pastime. Weather grows very warm and debilitating, and disinclines one for any active service of any sort. Goods have arrived at Fort Bliss from Victoria.

Wednesday, 14 May 1862

Received today the clothing, and the boxes were opened; numerous packages were directed to individuals and a quantity of clothing sent to the Company. I received two or three packages, touching though useful reminders of dear ones at home. I receive them with pride and delight. I feel proud to be thus convinced that though a stranger when I came to Victoria, with no fame or fortune or acquaintance, that I had made friends in two short years who, expecting no return, have kindly provided for my bodily comfort while I am in circumstances where I am in a great measure unable to do it myself. Lura Case sent me a great roll of linen bandages; Lucy Davies a pair socks and a comfort. Mrs. Davies a large bed quilt, most welcome of all. M. D. [Mary Dunbar] 2 pair socks and a comfort, besides a *comfortable* little note in the interior. M. G. [Marion Goodwin] sent me a substantial pair of socks, my name on one side of the card and hers beneath on the other side. God bless

---

99. Upon arrival in Franklin, the guns of McRae's Battery were assigned to a newly organized unit called the Valverde Battery. Commanded by Capt. Joseph D. Sayres, later governor of Texas, the Valverde Battery fought with the Sibley Brigade throughout the rest of the Civil War. Peticolas often mentions the battery in the third volume of his wartime journal. (Hall, *Confederate Army of New Mexico*, p. 289.)

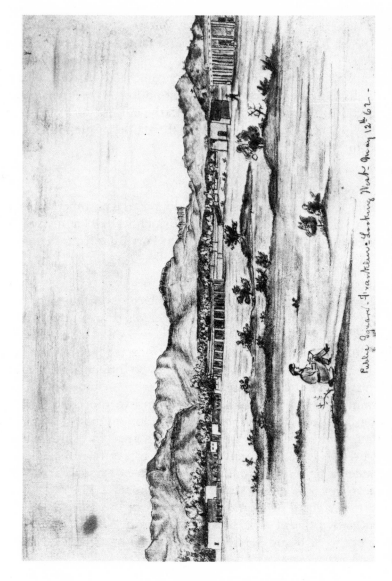

Public Square—Franklin, Looking West May 12th 62 –

"Public Square—Franklin, Looking West, May 12th 1862." Now the downtown plaza of El Paso, Texas, with artist shown in foreground. (Arizona Historical Society)

130

her!! M. C. [?], another of my lady friends, sent the same articles, card, and name in the same manner.

Mrs. Shirkey sent me two pair socks; good substantial articles. Besides these things I drew of the Company donations 1 blanket, 1 pair pants, 1 heavy shirt, and 2 pair socks, so I am now well supplied in socks at least. I gave Lytle a pair of socks as I did not need all I had. Went down to the river this evening, took a thorough bath, and put on clean clothes out and out. What a luxury! May heaven bless our friends in Victoria. John Kuykendall has broken out finally with the measles and will doubtless get well in a few days. There were 9 fine *Sombrero* hats sent up; of these, Fenner got one, Linn one, Bart one, Al Field one, Coon [S. S. or Thomas A.] Field one, and the rest were drawn by different members of the Company. If all were drawn for as they should have been, it is singular indeed that 2 Lieuts., the new Capt'n., and the orderly should have all drawn lucky numbers one after the other in quick succession. If they were not drawn for but merely *appropriated* by those officers, then they have done something they had no right to do, as the hats were sent as much to one man as another, and by a fair lottery every man ought to have had a chance to draw a hat. When we are paid off we can perhaps buy hats.

Thursday, 15 May 1862

Laid in camp today, as idle as usual. I got hold of Ike Marvel's "Reveries of a Bachelor" and read it with great interest though I have read it before.

Friday, 16 May 1862

Wrote to Dr. Davies today, and a note of thanks to S. A. White for publication in behalf of the company.[100] We have been eating light bread for a week. I am the maker. We bake and rise it, for want of an oven, in a messpan. The bread is very good indeed. We merely keep a small lump of the dough after we make up a batch, to work in with the next baking, and thus have the rising all the time.

Saturday, 17 May 1862

Coffee is still busy making out the muster and pay rolls. This is a tedious job, as four copies of each have to be made out. Clark

---

100. This was Samuel A. White, Peticolas's law partner and editor of the *Victoria Advocate*.

died on Thursday and we buried him yesterday. Purcell and Kleberg are sick; Purcell has yellow jaunders [*sic*]. Clark died with billious fever and the yellow jaunders combined. All the men are more or less unwell, and it is distressing to notice how general is the debility in camp. Gambling is extensively practiced by the troops that have been paid off, and large sums in Confederate notes change hands here daily over the gambling tables. Guard has been pretty much discontinued. John Kuykendall has joined my mess. We now number 5. John is getting better but is not well yet. Roeder is still sick.

Sunday, 18 May 1862

Went down to the German Company,[101] 3/4 of a mile below Bliss today, and copied a number of sketches from a book that a member of that Company has, containing up-country sketches: "The graves at Val Verde;" Churches in Alberkirque, Santa Fe, and various other places; "The 1st Regt. Crossing the river below Alberkirque;" etc. I found Companies E and G camped in a pleasant cottonwood grove and their health has been much better than ours.

Monday, 19 May 1862

I finished up some of the sketches I took yesterday and read a good deal in the "History of the French Revolution," a large volume of some 1800 pages. In the evening I took a nap and then got supper. [B. A.] Jones is sick. News we got by Sunday evening's mail is of a mixed character. [Gen. Don Carlos] Buell and his Tennessee Army have evacuated Nashville and our troops are there. The Federal Army is completely disorganized and has a great Number of sick: 14,000 men left in Nashville. The Abs admit the loss of 18,000 in killed, wounded, and prisoners from the Battle of Shiloah. Their gunboats have succeeded in passing the forts below New Orleans on the Miss—— River and are now lying before the city, which has been evacuated by our troops who, 60,000 strong, are lying outside the city. Abs demanded a surrender of the mayor, who refused to make it and told them that if they wanted to land and take possession to do so. They have not yet landed.[102]

---

101. Company G, First Regiment, was almost entirely composed of Dutch and German settlers from Austin, Washington, and Fayette counties. Several of these copied sketches are reproduced herein. (Hall, *Confederate Army of New Mexico*, p. 99.)

102. The Federal fleet commanded by Flag Officer David G. Farragut took possession of New Orleans, without its formal surrender, on 25 April 1862.

"Hospital, C. S. A. Franklin, May 19th '62." Peticolas's sketch of this facility after the Sibley Brigade returned from New Mexico. (Arizona Historical Society)

Tuesday, 20 May 1862

Drew in my sketch book today. Jones is too sick to do anything atall. John Kuykendall is getting better. Purcell has gone to the hospital to be a regular attendant. Lytle is complaining. Major Hampton is recovering. I took a sketch of the CSA Hospital here this morning. It is a fine building. The talk in camp now is of our going down to San Antonio soon—across the plains on foot!! George Harpoldt is getting ready to bake bread and will begin tomorrow. We were notified tonight that tomorrow is pay day and requested to get our breakfast early, as we have to go down to the post.

Wednesday, 21 May 1862

We signed the pay roll this morning and went down to the post to draw our pay. We received 3 months' and 20 days' pay, amounting with most of the men to $96.80. I received $115.13 pay as a sergeant. I paid [Lt. James B.] Holland $20 on my note drawn in his favor for $100, part pay for my mule *Lucy Shaw*. I purchased this evening $2.00 worth of black pepper. On the opposite page I have pasted the General's address to his men. It is a curious specimen of literature in some respects.

Thursday, 22 May 1862

Laid over today and did a little of everything and not a great deal of anything. I read a little, wrote a letter, and finished up some of my sketches, and part of the time I sat and reflected upon the different characters and dispositions of different members of our Company. The most striking one among the Germans, [Gideon] Egg, is a rapid talker and vehement in all his actions, with a peculiarity of emphasis that distinguishes him from all others. He is kind in his disposition and possesses considerable quickness of perception. Johnny [John W.] Owens, a native of the Emerald Isles, is a man of low stature and rugged countenance, with a decided partiality for whiskey, an enthusiastic admiration of everything Irish and of Irishmen generally, and a bitter hatred for Aristocracy, which he affirms he is fighting against in the North, sufficient brogue and irish humor to render him interesting, and is in fact a character which a Dickens might delineate and illustrate so as to be quite interesting. [Gustavus] Dietze, a German of quiet and retiring disposition, of good manners and tolerable education, with high cheek bones and prominent nose, but rapid in action and words when roused, is another character. Then there is John Schmidt, the oracle of his mess, a man

SOLDIERS OF THE ARMY OF NEW MEXICO.

It is with unfeigned pride and pleasure that I find myself occupying a position which devolves upon me the duty of congratulating the Army of New Mexico upon the successes which have crowned their arms in the many encounters with the enemy during the short but brilliant campaign which has just terminated.

Called from your homes almost at a moment's warning, cheerfully leaving friends, families and private affairs, in many cases solely dependent upon your presence and personal attention, scarcely prepared for a month's campaign, in the immediate defence of your own firesides, you have made a march, many of you of over a thousand miles, before ever reaching the field of active operations.

The boasted valor of TEXANS has been fully vindicated. VALVERDE, Glorietta, Albuquerque, Peralto, and last, though not least, your successful and almost unprecedented evacuation, through mountain passes and over a trackless waste of a hundred miles through a famishing country, will be duly chronicled, and form one of the brightest pages in the history of the Second American Revolution.

That I should be proud of you—that every participant in the campaign should be proud of himself—who can doubt?

During the short period of inaction which you are now enjoying, your General indulges the hope that you will constantly bear in mind, that at any moment you may be recalled into activity.

God and an indulgent Providence have guided us in our councils and watched our ways: let us be thankful to Him for our successes, and to Him let not forget to offer a prayer for our noble dead.

H. H. SIBLEY,
BRIG. GEN. COMMANDING

Proclamation issued to his men by General Sibley while they were resting and refitting in Franklin, Texas, in preparation for leaving New Mexico. (Peticolas Journal)

who has been in European service and to whom it is impossible to apply for any information but what he will attempt to give it, profoundly versed in war, politics, and religion. He talks incessantly when started, and lays down his opinions to the Germans and Irish as one would enunciate an axiom in mathematics. He is the arbiter of all disputes amongst the Germans, and whether the question concerns the idiom of a language, the usage of a certain nation, the government of an Army, or the right way to bake bread, he lays down his law, asked or unasked. Add to this, he is fond of manufacturing facts. Then, [Philip] Meyer is another character of singular idiosyncracies. He is a youngster of 20, has a deep scar on his cheek from the corner of the mouth downwards, round head, round face, little prominence of features, is a *good* singer, a first-rate mimic, a great jester, and has a great deal of pig-headedness when he determines upon any given line of action or upon carrying an end. He is free of speech and is quite interesting; in some of his moods is playfull and full of life and fun.

There are many others who have peculiarities, but none so very prominent as these, but enough to give any one considerable insight into human nature who has time and inclination to watch them in all their developments. R. Purcell, for instance, is very wordy and fond of argument, but frequently loses its drift, gets mentally befogged, and then works his way out by abusing his opponent and his opponent's ideas. I have frequently amused and interested [myself] in watching and reading characters by the light of actions and conversation.

Friday, 23 May 1862

Went over to El Paso [Ciudad Juarez] today. The wind was high and the waves considerable, and our little Canoe rocked considerably, but there was no danger of a ducking atall. We passed through a mile of suburbs, which is much more attractive than the city itself. Extensive vineyards, all green and in full leaf, are planted along in the river bottom, varied by wheat fields just heading out. There, every *Saco* was full and every one of them has a row of trees on each side, large green cottonwoods.[103] Neat adobe dwellings nestle away amongst the trees and vines, almost hidden from view, and to the hot footman the shade looks very inviting. Large orchards, too, are

---

103. This was the same term used by the Texans in the upper Rio Grande Valley, a corruption of *acéquia*, or irrigation ditch.

numerous and every variety of fruit is plentiful. Peaches, apples, and quinces are as large as your thumb, and cherries, plums, and other small fruit in abundance. Adobe walls 4 or five feet high divide different fields and different possessions. The town is not very fine but is extensive. I made a few purchases and took a sketch of the Church in the main Plaza. While I was busy working on the sketch, sitting in the shadow of the colonnade fronting the Church, quite a number of Mexicans surrounded me with exclamations of "Carramba!" "Muncha bonita!!" "Esta bueno" etc., etc., while one old fellow with a tremendous sombrero and a stick acted as master of the assembly and kept them out of my way by gestures and talk. Their unintelligible jabber amused me (formerly it would have annoyed), and I worked away quite regardless of the spectators. I took another sketch in the rear of the town, as I returned toward the river, of the first view of the town. Here I was entertained by a little Mexican boy who talked to me with great animation in the musical tones of his national language, and he even fancied that he was interesting me vastly until my "no comprendo Senior" threw a damper upon his feelings. He was evidently considerably excited by seeing me drawing El Paso, and from what I could understand, he wanted me to put him down on paper too. I got back to Quarters about 2 P.M. and ate a hearty meal of tea, sugar mince, and bread and beef.

This is all we have to eat now. Harpoldt, baker, bakes bread for the 2 Companies here, and we buy the tea at $3.00 per pound in El Paso. Everything costs 3 prices in paper in El Paso, and we hardly have money enough to pay for things we are compelled to have on the road to San Antonio, where it seems we are all going soon if all reports are true. Words can hardly express how much I dread to undertake to walk across that vast desert region between Ft. Quitman and Ft. Clark. It was hard enough riding it in the fall, but walking it in the blazing suns of a torrid summer, it will be infinitely worse. Numbers will give out on the road, numbers will stop at the posts, too sick to go on, and when we reach San Antonio the brigade will be dwindled to a regiment.

Saturday, 24 May 1862

Nothing unusual occurred today. We still hear of our expected move but don't know when we will start. [Fridolin] Roth and [A.] Goldman have made money since we have been here, Roth by baking and selling pies, Goldman by purchasing such articles as we most

"Church in El Paso, May 22nd '62." Peticolas's sketch of the plaza and church in present-day Ciudad Juarez. (Arizona Historical Society)

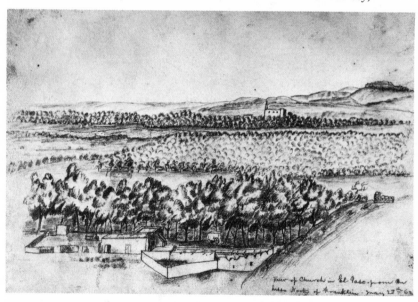

"View of Church in El Paso from the hills North of Franklin, May 27th '62." Peticolas's sketch of the area that is now downtown El Paso, Texas, looking south to the church in Ciudad Juarez. (Arizona Historical Society)

need in El Paso and selling them here at an enormous profit—wine, waterkegs, (*poloynseys*) [*piloncillos:* hard Mexican sugar candies]— don't know whether spelling is correct or not—chocolate, etc. A good many of the boys have spent 20 $ in wine alone with him, $5 per bottle.

Sunday, 25 May 1862

News by mail today is that two decisive battles have been fought by [Gen. P. G. T.] Beauregard and Joe [Gen. Joseph E.] Johnston, in both of which the Confederate arms have been victorious, and that the army of Tennessee is marching on St. Louis and the army of the Potomac upon Washington.[104]

Monday, 26 May 1862

Nothing has happened today worthy of note. I amused myself drawing a sketch of our passage through the Mountains around Craig.

Tuesday, 27 May 1862

Today I complete my 23rd year. My birthday has come once more and I look back with interest upon a not uneventful life. Changes which I had never dreamt of have happened to me, dangers that I never anticipated have encompassed me, and for the last 8 months I have encountered the severest hardships that I have ever experienced; but it is with satisfaction that I make a review of the past, for I have no crimes to look back upon which would fill me with remorse. Errors that I have committed I can see easily, and regrets sometimes fill my mind when I look back and mark the points upon my path when, had I adopted a different course from the one I did pursue, my circumstances might have been very different from what they now are; but then the mind grows bewildered in trying to solve the *"might have been"* and no one can tell where our untrod path would have led to.

---

104. This was faulty news. During early May, Beauregard fought the Federal forces slowly advancing toward Corinth, Mississippi, gradually falling back to that city, then evacuating it on 30 May. On Virginia's Peninsula, Johnston had also fallen back before the Federal army moving toward Richmond, but did not engage in any significant fighting until the Battle of Seven Pines on 31 May. No Confederate armies were marching on either St. Louis or Washington, although Gen. Thomas J. Jackson's Shenandoah Valley campaign was often seen as threatening the capital.

Wednesday, 28 May 1862

Franklin is an interesting place on some accounts. The scenes that are daily met with here, and the peculiar habits of its present inhabitants form interesting subjects to an inquiring mind, and while there is nothing transpiring to rouse to painful or passionate activities, there is enough to interest and amuse. The bridge across the *saco* is the market-place of the town. Here the copper-colored Mexicans with their broad-brim sombreros bring their baskets with lettuce, onions, (Poloynseys), and little mince pies, and to this place the soldiers saunter during the morning to trade old clothes, meat, or shoes or (paper) for the various articles exhibited for sale. Here, too, the sentinel with his gun is posted as a sort of police guard to maintain inviolate the quiet of the town, and happily, he seldom has any thing to do. Then there are the gambling saloons, a decided feature in the *tout ensemble* of the town, and though I never gamble, I sometimes visit these rooms and look on and see money change hands, and it introduces me to a long string of semi-philosophic, semi-moral reflections upon this singular passion.

Thursday, 29 May 1862

There is some talk today of a flatboat expedition to Ft. Quitman to take down rations, and a detail to take the boat down is being made. The boat is to be piloted by a man who has been a resident citizen and boatman here for several years. News from above is that a company of the 3rd Regiment consisting of 140 men has behaved most *heroically* in a little affair with the enemy lately. It deserves being recorded and preserved. A few days ago the 3rd Regiment was ordered to drive in the enemy's pickets towards Craig; 140 in command of a captain and a due number of Lieutenants went up. Captain got sick and left 1st. Lieut. in command. They went up to a little town near Craig [Paraje] where we crossed the river going up. Their spies went into town one night, found 80 Federals with 220 head of horses and mules in their charge in the town. They had no picket or camp guard and were all wrapped in slumber. Nothing could have been more easily accomplished than to have surrounded and made them all prisoners and taken all the stock. The river was too high to admit of their retreating to Craig, or receiving from thence any reinforcement. The spy returned to the command and informed the Lieut. Commanding of the state of things, but he refused to act that night and sent a man in the next morning with a flag of truce to demand a surrender. The bearer of the flag went in, roused the

140

Federal Commander, and demanded a surrender. The Ab captain replied that he would surrender if they had enough men. Then this redoubtable 1st. Lieut. drew his men up in line of battle to *take the vote* whether they should attack the enemy or *retire*. They were in about 800 yards of the town. The Federals, seeing them in line of battle, opened upon them with their minie muskets, and the noble men did not wait to vote upon the question submitted but retreated precipitately and returned to Steele's camp.[105]

Friday, 30 May 1862

Nothing going on today of any particular importance. I learned something today that I did not know before. 1st, that on the 16th Feb'y 62, Sunday, when we returned from our reconnoitering and skirmish near Craig, that Green and his Regiment did not camp that night with the 1st and 3rd Regt., but went back to his old camp 5 miles further from Craig and was ordered back to us the same night, and reached us about daybreak on the morning of the 17th. 2nd, that on the 17th April in the Council of War held at the camp when we left the river to retreat through the Mountains, that Scurry was

---

105. The operation to which Peticolas refers was a horse-stealing raid against Canby's herd, which was kept on the east side of the Rio Grande at the tiny village of Paraje de Fray Cristobal, eight miles below Fort Craig. Selecting the 100 best-mounted men from among the six relatively fresh companies of the Third Regiment that had remained in the Mesilla Valley, Colonel Steele sent them northward from Doña Ana on 19 May to capture the Union horses. Capt. Thomas O. Moody, Co. K, led the expedition, but soon became ill from drinking bad water, and command of the detachment passed to Lt. Isaac G. Bowman of the same company. His path was along the nearly waterless Jornada del Muerto, a ninety-mile shortcut on the Santa Fe–Chihuahua trade route, which had Paraje as its northern terminus. Arriving near Paraje early on the morning of 21 May, rather than immediately attacking, as ordered, Bowman sent messengers into the Federal camp to demand its surrender. With forty-five men and two cannons, the Union commander refused and challenged Bowman to "Come on, that he would fight a string before surrendering." Bowman thereupon lost heart, declared "Boys, the jig is up. We have no artillery," and immediately led his command back toward Doña Ana. One of the Texans, Private Felix R. Collard, volunteered to return with a small group under Lt. Wiley Robin to fight the Federals. Both sides exchanged a brief fire, but a round of grape shot or canister balls from one of the Federal cannons convinced this little band to retreat also, thus ending in embarrassment for the Confederates the last actual skirmish of the New Mexico campaign. Collard, along with many of his companions whose horses gave out on the blistering Jornada ("Horn Alley" to the Texans), struggled southward, barely surviving the raid. Of Lieutenant Bowman, Collard wrote: "To know that the Confederacy had such a commissioned officer makes me blush with shame." (*O.R.* IX: 608; Felix R. Collard, "Reminiscences of a Private, Company 'G,' 7th Texas Cavalry, Sibley Brigade, CSA," 1922, MSS. Original in collection of Dr. Robert F. Collard of Albuquerque. Typescript in editor's collection.)

called on for his opinion but refused to give it atall. Sibley, so [Lt. Philip] Fulcrod says, was in favor of going on down the river. Green, Coopwood, and [Lt. Col. Henry C.] McNeill preferred the mountain route, and Scurry was silent.

Saturday, 31 May 1862

I was on the detail to go down to Quitman on the flat[boat], and I went down and reported this evening to Colonel Hardeman. Charlie Linn was placed in command of the men, and we were required to go down in the morning to attend to the loading. I came back to Franklin this evening and staid all night at our quarters.

Sunday, 1 June 1862

News of Beauregard's and Joe Johnston's victories is in a measure confirmed. Nothing going on in camp. Preparations still going on for our trip down the river. We were with the flatboat all day and got it loaded with 200 sacks of flour. When we got it loaded, the boat sprung a leak and we had to take out the flour as rapidly as possible to prevent the boat from sinking. This was severe work, and before we could get it all out about 60 sacks got wet, but not enough to damage it much. Thus our flatboat expedition was brought to a close. I slept down at the boat tonight, and supped on bread and water, the same fare that I had had for dinner and breakfast. We have had nothing but bread and a little poor beef ever since we have been here, and such slim diet has reduced the men considerably, but I weigh the same I did in San Antonio (183 lbs) and have to thank a kind Providence for the blessing.

Monday, 2 June 1862

I came back to quarters this morning and staid in camp all day reading and drawing.

Tuesday, 3 June 1862

Nothing of interest occurring today.

Wednesday, 4 June 1862

I amused myself with my sketchbook and the History of the French Revolution. [Robert D.] Tippett brought over two Sombreros from El Paso today. Jno. Kuykendall bought one at $10.00.

Thursday, 5 June 1862

Tomorrow is fixed for the day of our departure from Franklin. Preparations are going on rapidly. Field's Company left yesterday. I went over to El Paso today and bought a Sombrero for $11.75, a black wool hat; and now I will give a sum of my expenses and payments since I have been here.

Paid on notes for Mule	$20.00
Paid Sutler in full	20.00
1 hat	11.75
1 keg for water	2.00
1 lb blk tea	3.00
5 spoons	1.00
4 lbs pepper	2.00
Tobacco	2.00

The above is about all, save some small sums for ferryage, pipes, etc.

Thursday, 5 June 1862 [second entry]

Lying in camp today. Our company is to start tomorrow evening.

Friday, 6 June 1862

We started this evening for the post, John Kuykendall and R. Purcell both having succeeded in getting four-footed beasts to ride. There will be only a few of our Company left. George Moody and [James M.] Mercer stay, as George is too unwell to travel. W. B. James purchased a horse today and will be able to go. We loaded up and went to the post this evening. Camped in the rear of the fort and staid all night. We have drawn 20 days' rations to last us till Ft. Davis. Transportation is extremely scarce, and I had to sell one of my blankets to make my baggage lighter, though it weighs very little.

Saturday, 7 June 1862

We made a late start this morning and traveled slowly on account of the sick, but succeeded by 5 in the evening in getting to San Isleta, on the confines of which town we formed our camp. The road though very level is sandy, and there is one very difficult crossing of a *saco* on the way, which is flooded by the rise in the river and is very boggy. Here our wagons were delayed an hour making the crossing. In spite of the distance traveled (12 miles and the

143

"San Isleta, June 9th." Sketched by Peticolas on the return trip the day after leaving Franklin, Texas. (Arizona Historical Society)

wading of the *saco*), all those who are unwell appear to be in better spirits and improving, and tonight all the sounds in camp intimate a fast recovering cheerfulness. Linn is laughing and joking his friends, Fenner congratulating himself on the cheerfulness of the camp; Roeder rousing himself from his usual profound apathy and indolence and summing up energy enough to cut his hay (green wheat) for his own horse, and broil a piece of beef. [E.] Powell is singing old-time baptist hymns, and the rich strains of some of the most celebrated German airs rise from the lower end of the company where the Germans are camped; tenor, soprano, bass, and all complete, and I sit here upon my outspread blankets just before retiring to rest, and scribble up my journal by the flickering light of a cottonwood brush camp-fire.

Sunday, 8 June 1862

Once more the day set apart for a rest from all our labors, the day of rest no longer. After having traveled six miles, I seat myself in the shadow of a willow tree and rest and muse upon the present, the past, the future. Time was when this day saw me cheerfully and happily wending my way to church, when time was more wont to hang heavily on my hands, when surrounded by friends and acquaintances, often times with the fairer sex I took part in the services and found pleasure in the place, my surroundings, and the occupation. Now it comes, tis true, once every seven days, but it no longer comes to give respite to toil; to revive and invigorate by rest the mind wearied by the incessant study of six days; no longer in its sweet pealing bells speaks of rest, of quiet, of a day given to different and better pursuits than those so eagerly followed during the six days—no longer brings a breathing time in which to review the past days and profit by the review. Tis true the bells may be heard; I heard them this morning while stopping to take a hasty sketch of Isleta. I heard them while passing through San Elizario, but though it brought to mind other days, as such sounds always do, it did not authorize me to stop, even if I had been inclined to halt and take part in a Catholic mummery in a language I do not understand; for the main body of the command had gone on. The order is March, and it becomes not a soldier to tarry, much less halt. Then I look forward earnestly into a future whose misty shrouds are all bloody and sad, to strive and divine when 'wars and tumult shall cease, and happiness and peace reign over all the world'!! Alas, alas!! the most hopeful prophet would be puzzled to find a base upon which

145

to predict its speedy coming. Capt. Crosson appointed me acting Sergeant Major for the rear division, and he says he thinks I will have to act to San Antonio. Thus I find myself upon extra duty.[106]

Monday, 9 June 1862

The wind blew pretty cold this morning and we made an early start. Traveled about 10 miles and made a halt at a stage stand on the way, and waited for the wagons to come up. When they arrived we moved on. We moved about a mile from the station stand till 3 or 4 P.M. in the evening and then moved on 3 miles further through very deep sand and camped for the night. The above sketch [Mountain Range in Mexico] I took from a point up the hill 3 miles further on than the place where we camped, from which hill we had to return when we heard the bugle sound the recall.[107]

Tuesday, 10 June 1862

Traveled 12 miles today, nooned, and camped as usual. Had some very fat beef today and made a pot of soup for dinner that we all relished exceedingly. The sick do not get much better, nor do their numbers diminish as I had hoped they would, but all are cheerful and are supported by the idea of getting home. The weather is warm and if it was not for the breeze we would suffer. The Rio Grande river well deserves its name; in places it is nearly a mile wide, and the water runs far out into the bottoms through the natural *sacos* that abound in the valleys.[108] This compels us to follow a circuitous route around on the hills, throws us out of the shade and into the sand, and renders our journey much more tedious and laborious than it would otherwise be. We had to push and pull our wagon this morning 2 or 3 miles through the heavy sand, and the number of sick renders it extremely laborious to those who are well, for they haven't the strength of the Company as we had in our retreat through the Mountains with the artillery.

---

106. Peticolas's camp was near the village of San Elizario, some twenty-five miles below Franklin.

107. This camp was in the vicinity of the village of Tornillo, Texas.

108. Runoff from the heavy, late-season snow in northern New Mexico had apparently put the Rio Grande over its normal banks and into the arroyos leading down to the river, flooding the road over which Peticolas had come north during the previous December. Company C camped near the village of Acala, Texas.

146

the near division & he says that
he thinks I will have to act to
San Antonio — Thus I find myself upon extra duty —

Monday 9th June 1862
The winds blew pritty cold this
morning and we made an
early start — traveled about 12
miles and made a halt at
a Stage stand on the way —
and waited for the wagons to
come up when they arrived we
moved on   towards San

Stage Station 12 miles from San
Elizario —
We are about a mile from the

"Stage Station 12 miles from San Elizario" 9 June 1862.
(Peticolas Journal)

"High Noon!! The *Siesta:* Lieut. R. Dreams of Glorietta!" Peticolas's sketch of Lt. Ludwig von Roeder, Co. C, Fourth Texas Mounted Volunteers, sleeping under a mesquite bush, shaded by his sombrero, 11 June 1862. (Peticolas Journal)

Wednesday, 11 June 1862

We passed through Smith's Ranch today and traveled about 10 miles before we nooned. We left a man at the ranch who had the smallpox, and from appearances, I shouldn't be surprised if we have a good many at Fort Quitman. We have heard of the taking of Norfolk, Va. and Galveston by the Abs. I have received, too, a letter from home giving me all the news. The letter is from Jennie.[109] Arthur Coleman, cousin, Adjutant of a Regiment in [Gen. John B.] Floyd's Brigade, was either killed or taken prisoner at Fort Donaldson [*sic*]. Ben Brown is 1st. Lieut in the Amherst C. H. Company. Gus (my brother) came home from the Campaign in Missouri where he was in the battles of Springfield, Lexington, and appears all well and sound; staid 2 months and then joined Whitehead's Cavalry Co. and went to Goodsonville. All well at home save Adolph; he hasn't recovered from the pneumonia contracted in Camp Manassas. Cousin Mollie had returned from Missouri; also, Vaughan is Col. in the Southern Army, and she has come home to stay till the war is over. We didn't move from our noon encampment, as we had to wait for Co. B, which had to wait for its flour, behind on Mexican carts.

Thursday, 12 June 1862

Traveled about 8 miles today, and camped for noon, then traveled some 5 or 6 miles further and camped for the night within about 14 miles of Ft. Quitman.

Friday, 13 June 1862

We traveled this morning through a very sandy road some 7 or 8 miles and camped in about 5 miles of Quitman. Here we remained all night and will stay tomorrow, as the 1st Division is at Quitman and we have to give them time to get away from Eagle Springs before we get there.[110] We have better grass up here than there is around Quitman, and this is the cause of our stay.

---

109. The writer was Peticolas's sister, Jennie R. Peticolas of Amherst Court House, Virginia.

110. The Sibley Brigade returned by the same Fort Bliss–San Antonio stage road they had used seven months earlier coming west. Again, the regiments marched in separate battalions in order to find sufficient water along the way. Pyron's battalion led the column, followed by a part of the First Regiment. Peticolas and Company C were in the next battalion, and were in turn followed by units of the Second Regiment. About half of the Third Regiment also left Franklin, but Colonel Steele remained behind with 400 men of that regiment to hold the Fort Bliss–Mesilla Valley area and

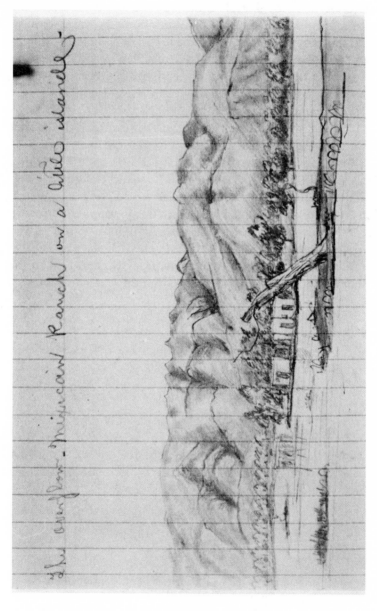

"The overflow. Mexican Ranch on a little island." View of the Rio Grande near Ft. Quitman during flood stage after heavy runoff from melting snows in New Mexico, 14 June 1862. (Peticolas Journal)

Saturday, 14 June 1862

We laid in camp today according to the programme and let our mules rest. I baked some very good lightbread today. [N. B.] Lytle went down to the 1st Division to try and get John Kuykendall's little grey mare that he heard was at that place, but came back late in the evening entirely unsuccessful, the man not being in that division. The 1st Division leaves this evening for the plains. I mounted guard as usual tonight and retired early. News by mail is that 7000 Federals have landed at Port Lavacca. This, however, is merely an item dropped by the driver, and we don't know whether or not it is reliable, as we haven't seen it in letter or paper.[111]

Sunday, 15 June 1862

We made a very early start this morning while the stars were yet shining and traveled to within 2 miles of where the road leaves the valley.[112] Then we camped about 10 o'clock and here we will remain till late this evening when we will travel the other two miles. I will consider the two miles already traveled and close my memoirs of another Sunday here. And now as I approach the end of another volume of my journal, and find the wish that I had written on the last page of my 1st book (that before I finished this one the war would be over) so far from being realized that the bloody drama on the western continent seems to be just fully opening, I cannot suppress a feeling of profound sadness. The end of a book, even though it be like this, but a journal of the acts of one man and that man the writer, affords a sort of breathing space, as with writers who

---

support the government of the Confederate Territory of Arizona. However, these plans soon went awry. By late June, General Canby had a 2,000-man field force available and planned to drive any remaining Rebels out of the Mesilla Valley and West Texas. Before he had time to act on his plans, however, he had unexpected reinforcements. From the Department of the Pacific, a column of 1,400 men with attached artillery had marched across the deserts of Arizona to Canby's assistance. Under Brig. Gen. James H. Carleton, this "California Column" reached the upper Mesilla Valley on 4 July 1862, uniting soon afterward with Canby's advance units. Knowing of the approach of both these strong Union forces, Colonel Steele evacuated Confederate Arizona and withdrew his last troops from the Fort Bliss area by 12 July, leaving only a military hospital for those Texan soldiers too sick to travel back to San Antonio. For a more complete history of Carleton's subsequent role in Civil War New Mexico, see Darlis A. Miller, *The California Column in New Mexico* (Albuquerque: University of New Mexico Press, 1982). (*O.R.* IX: 678–80, 686–88.)

111. The news was not reliable; Port Lavaca was not attacked until the U.S. Navy bombarded it on 31 October 1862.

112. This camp was about five miles south of Fort Quitman.

regulate the size of their volumes, a time which marks an *epoch* in the history they are writing, and a new volume of my work written after this plan generally marks a new era in the course of the nation or the individual whose history is being written, and now upon the eve of again undertaking that long journey of 650 miles from the river Rio Grande to the city of San Antonio across the vast elevated plains, the world of the wandering indian tribes, with but little water and no wood; now as I with the regiment undertake this journey on foot and in the heat of summer, I deem this an era in the history of my first 12 months in the service of the Confederate States of sufficient importance to warrant me in bringing this volume to a close, this time without expressing a wish or making a prediction. Providence, who ruleth all things, can alone bring this war to a speedy conclusion and deliver us from its evils, its distresses, its blood, its destructiveness.

End of Vol. 2nd.

Epilogue

As A. B. Peticolas and his companions left New Mexico, many of them were disgusted with the conduct of the campaign and with their commanding general. One Second Regiment soldier observed, "It seems too bad that after enduring so much in this country that we will be obliged to leave it—starved out—not run out. . . . It can never be said that the unfortunate result of this campaign was caused by any *failure* on the part of *the soldiers*. . . ." However, he added, "everyone detests the country so much that they are really glad to go, for we all think that our operations out here will all be lost in history, when such great struggles are going on nearer home. . . ."[1] Capt. Jerome B. McCown, of the same regiment, expressed similar feelings in a letter to the editor of the Bellville, Texas, newspaper. "We are all tired of this country," he said, and "are all anxious to return to the sunny land of Texas. . . ." Once there, the captain felt, the brigade members would be defending their homes and families and not "throwing our lives away in endeavoring to obtain possession of a country which is not worth the life of one good man, of the many who have breathed their last on its arid sands."[2]

The arid sands of New Mexico seemed almost hospitable, however, compared to the scorched plains of West Texas, as the Sibley Brigade marched eastward. The route retraced their earlier outbound journey along the Fort Bliss–San Antonio stage road, and

---

1. Starr Campaign Letters, p. 187.

2. Capt. J. B. McCown, Co. G, Fifth Texas, to editor, *Countryman*, 6 May 1862, in *The Bellville Countryman* (Texas), 7 June 1862.

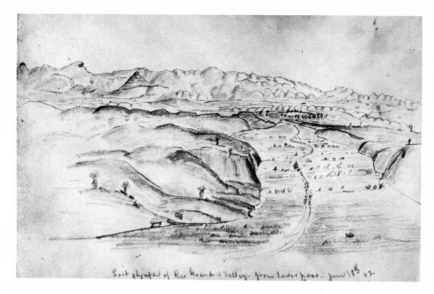

"Last glimpse of Rio Grande & valley, from lower pass, June 17th '62."
The Confederate column is shown ascending the slope leading to Eagle
Springs from the river bottom south of Fort Quitman, Texas, on the
journey to San Antonio. (Arizona Historical Society)

"Gateway to the Plains & Lower Pass, Looking west, 17 June '62."
Peticolas is shown sketching the Confederate journey along the stage
road leading to Eagle Springs. (Arizona Historical Society)

Peticolas's dread at undertaking such a trip during midsummer proved well founded. Each day's march soon degenerated into a struggle to reach the meager water available along the way. In addition, the companies were harassed by Indians who ran off livestock and polluted wells. After passing through Forts Davis and Stockton, Peticolas and Company C reached the Pecos River on the last day of June, then crossed to Devil's River and were nearing "civilization" at Fort Clark two weeks later. On 19 July, he was once again back in San Antonio. The First Regiment briefly went into camp at the Salado Creek training area east of San Antonio, but the men were almost immediately given sixty-day furloughs so that they could rest and reequip themselves at home.[3] Consequently, Peticolas was back in Victoria by late July 1862, staying at the Shirkey House and renewing his acquaintance with the young ladies of the town.[4]

For the "Victoria Invincibles," the New Mexico campaign had resulted in significant losses. Of the eighty soldiers of Company C who had actually participated in operations north of the Mesilla Valley, three were killed and ten severely wounded in battle. In addition, fourteen were captured and two died of disease during the campaign, for a total casualty rate of 36 percent. However, most of the healthy prisoners were exchanged and had returned to Texas by September 1862.[5]

The Sibley Brigade as a whole also suffered heavily. Of the approximately 3,200 troops that composed the Confederate Army of New Mexico around Fort Bliss during the winter of 1861–62, about 500 deserters, stragglers, and wounded Texans became Union prisoners. Because of both combat and disease, approximately 500 of the invading Confederates died.[6] Many paroled and exchanged prisoners subsequently rejoined the brigade, of course, but nevertheless, the price paid for this unfortunate campaign was high.

While the New Mexico campaign was barren of tangible results for the Confederacy, it was a source of lifetime pride for its partici-

3. Giesecke Diary, entries for 16 June–20 July 1862; Noel, *A Campaign from Santa Fe to the Mississippi*, pp. 51–54.

4. Alfred B. Peticolas, "Journal by A. B. Peticolas, Sergt, Co. C, 4th Regt. TMV, 12 September 1862–26 October 1863," MSS, in the collection of W. C. Peticolas of El Paso, Texas, entry for 12 September 1862. This is the third and final volume of Peticolas's wartime journal, hereafter cited as Peticolas Journal, 3.

5. Hall, *Confederate Army of New Mexico*, p. 76.

6. Hall, *Sibley's New Mexico Campaign*, pp. 202–3.

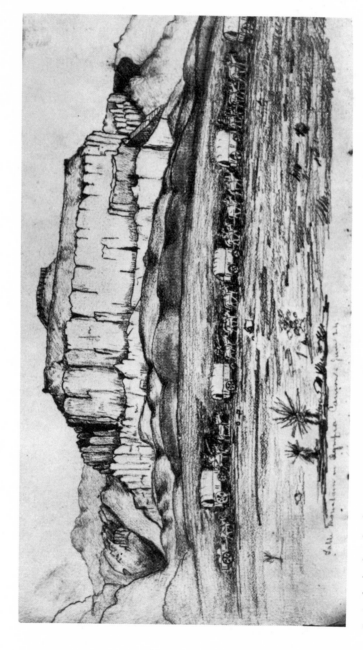

Peticolas's sketch of a retreating column of Texans passing Star Mountain, eleven miles northeast of Ft. Davis, Texas. (Arizona Historical Society)

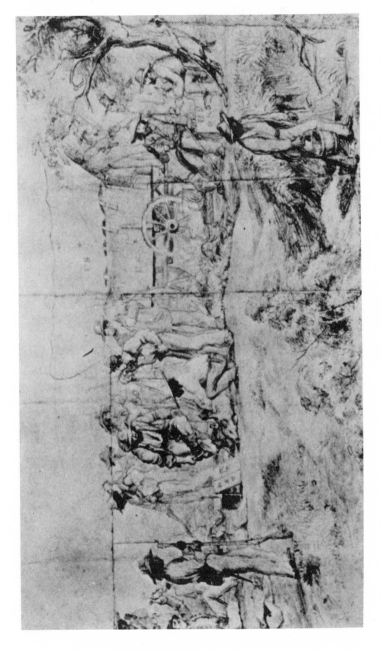

Confederate camp near Ft. Clark, Texas, ca. 1861. Sketch by Carl von Iwonski. (Editor's Collection)

pants. Although most of the Sibley Brigade fought through much larger and more significant battles throughout the remaining Civil War years, they tended to remember and cherish this first great military adventure above all others. For many of the young soldiers (the average age of Company C privates was twenty-three years),[7] their initial taste of danger and hardship in a distant and desolate land was impressive indeed. One of Peticolas's mess-mates, Thomas M. Field, even named his daughter, born nine years after the campaign, Glorieta ValVerde Field.[8]

Tales of New Mexico undoubtedly occupied much of the furlough time granted to Peticolas and his companions, but late summer 1862 soon brought a return to active duty. On 12 September he again bade farewell to his Victoria friends and rode toward the Company C rendezvous at Millican Bend, on the Brazos River. Unfortunately, military operations in Texas were almost as chaotic and disorganized as they had been a year earlier, with Confederate officials unable efficiently to control the movements of, or supply, the many units scattered about the countryside. As a result, Company C was sent home to await further orders. Peticolas returned to Victoria two days after he had left, thoroughly soaked by heavy showers en route. Over a month passed before he again said his farewells, leaving his adopted town for the Brazos River encampment.[9]

During November 1862, Peticolas served as acting sergeant major once the First Regiment concentrated at Millican Bend. Although the position was one of considerable prestige, and he seems to have really wanted it on a permanent basis, he claimed, "I hardly gave a penny, however, for the difference between my present position and that of S.M., as there is only $4. per month difference in the pay, and there is a great deal more than the worth of $4. per month in trouble." The permanent sergeant major subsequently reclaimed his position, but through Colonel Reily's influence Peticolas was named quartermaster sergeant of the First Regiment on 8 December. In that capacity, involving considerable responsibility and almost unrelieved toil, he served for a year with the Sibley Brigade.[10]

---

7. Hall, *Confederate Army of New Mexico*, pp. 77–80.

8. Pedigree Chart and Peticolas Family Genealogy, Merrow E. Sorley, comp. Copy in editor's collection.

9. Peticolas Journal, 3, entries for 12 September–23 October 1862.

10. Ibid., entries for 5, 10–13, 16, 17 November and 8 December 1862.

Peticolas's duties as quartermaster sergeant involved locating, purchasing, and forwarding to the First Regiment food for the men and fodder for the horses. To do so, he was usually away from the regiment. As a result, he missed much of the actual fighting, such as that in which detachments of the First Regiment participated during the Confederate land and sea attack on Federal naval units at Galveston on 1 January 1863.[11]

Peticolas was able, however, to join the First Regiment during its first battles with Union forces in Louisiana. During the second week of March 1863, General Sibley brought his entire brigade, 1,300 strong, into Opelousas, Louisiana, to join Gen. Richard Taylor's Confederate force opposing Federal troops west of New Orleans.[12] When these men, under Gen. Nathaniel P. Banks, moved westward in early April, Taylor fought a delaying action at Camp Bisland, southeast of Franklin, Louisiana, on 12 April. Peticolas and several companions had brought the regimental supply train into camp on the morning of the battle, then joined Company C on the field, where they deployed as skirmishers on the left of the Confederate line. Under Colonel Reily's command, the First Regiment fell back slowly before the advancing Federals, then stabilized their position behind a line of prepared breastworks. Fighting again flared along this position the following morning, but the First Regiment was withdrawn and galloped to the rear to oppose a landing by Union forces that outflanked the Bisland positions. Peticolas skirmished with the enemy all that day and retreated with his regiment into Franklin after dark, owing to what he believed to be a false alarm that the Texans were faced by overwhelming infantry forces.[13]

On the following morning, 14 April 1863, Peticolas fought in the Battle of Franklin, as Colonel Reily's small force held back the flanking enemy troops so that the balance of Taylor's Confederates could escape westward into south-central Louisiana, around New Iberia. The action was a success, but Reily was killed in the battle line,

11. Ibid., entry for 1 January 1863; Noel, *A Campaign from Santa Fe to the Mississippi*, pp. 64–67.

12. Richard Taylor, *Destruction and Reconstruction: Personal Experiences of the Late War*, Richard B. Howell, ed. (1879; reprint ed., New York: Longmans, Green and Co., 1955), p. 149. This work, by the commander of the Confederate District of Western Louisana, and son of President Zachary Taylor, is the best source for the 1863 and 1864 Red River campaigns, in which the Sibley Brigade participated.

13. Peticolas Journal, 3, entry for 1 May 1863; Noel, *A Campaign from Santa Fe to the Mississippi*, pp. 69–71.

Louisiana 1863–64

ARKANSAS

Shreveport

LOUISIANA

Vicksburg

Mansfield

Pleasant
Hill

Red River

MISSISSIPPI

Sabine River

Mississippi River

Alexandria

TEXAS

Cheneyville

Washington *Bayou Fordoche*

Opelousas

Bayou Teche

Atchafalaya River

Baton Rouge

Vermillionville

New Iberia

Franklin

New Orleans

Gulf of Mexico

Brashear City

Camp Bisland

0   50
miles

being succeeded in command of the First Regiment by Lt. Col. William P. Hardeman.[14]

Command of the First Cavalry Brigade, as the Sibley Brigade was formally designated, also changed. For whatever reason (Taylor said it was due to "feeble health"), General Sibley was placed in command of the baggage trains during the retreat from Bisland, while Colonel Green commanded Taylor's cavalry forces. Afterwards, Taylor preferred charges of disobedience and unofficerlike conduct against Sibley. Those charges resulted in a court-martial which found him not guilty, but nevertheless echoed Taylor's low opinion of his generalship. Sibley was not restored to command, and Green replaced him at the head of the brigade, which was thereafter known as Green's Brigade.[15]

Under General Tom Green, Peticolas fought as part of the rear guard of Taylor's army as it retreated northwestward toward Opelousas. On 17 April, he took part in a daylong skirmish with pursuing Federals at Vermillion Bayou and was almost captured when the retreating Confederates left him behind as he slept on the picket line after the day's fighting. Not only was he left behind, but his horse Silver, for which Peticolas had paid $400 on the way into Louisiana, and which he greatly cherished, was taken. Although Peticolas searched through the herds and camps of the other cavalry regiments when he rejoined the brigade, he never recovered the expensive mount.[16]

The exertions of constant travel to procure forage for the First Regiment, combined with his recent combat experiences, began to take their toll on Sergeant Peticolas's health. He was ill for a week during late April, and the illness returned during August 1863. Following another Confederate thrust toward New Orleans and a subsequent retreat to Washington, Louisiana, during which he was almost continuously on the move, the young forage master was again sick. In mid-August he wrote, "I was compelled to live a good deal on green corn and crackers, which gave me the diarrhea from which I have not yet entirely recovered."[17]

---

14. Peticolas Journal, 3, entry for 1 May 1863; Taylor, *Destruction and Reconstruction*, pp. 158–59; Noel, *A Campaign from Santa Fe to the Mississippi*, p. 153.

15. *O.R.* XV: 1093–96; Noel, *A Campaign from Santa Fe to the Mississippi*, pp. xvii, 78.

16. Peticolas Journal, 3, entries for 2 March and 1 May 1863.

17. Ibid., entry for 30 August 1863.

After participating in yet another attack against Union forces at Bayou Fordoche on 29 September, during which the First Regiment suffered from successive cold, drizzly days, Peticolas rode back to the Washington quartermaster depot with a severe fever and reported that "I could just get up stairs to [Capt. William H.] Harrison's office where I threw myself on a bed and stayed there until night, sending my horse back to camp." That action was unfortunate, for the horse, purchased to replace Silver, was stolen before Peticolas returned to the regimental camp. "It is a heavy loss to me," he wrote, "as I cannot replace him for less than $600, the price of Rat. I have bought him [Rat] and hope that he will not get lost too. I have now lost two fine horses in La. and am quite discouraged with my bad luck."[18]

By late October, Union thrusts had forced Green's men back northward as far as Cheneyville, Louisiana. There Peticolas became "very feeble from my fever and a return of my diarrhea" and relinquished the position of regimental forage master. He applied for a furlough and, in early November 1863, left the brigade to return to Texas.[19]

Green's Brigade fought on throughout the 1864 Red River campaign, performing with distinction at the battles of Mansfield and Pleasant Hill, where General Green was killed on 9 April. During December 1864, the brigade returned to Texas and served out the remaining months of the Civil War in that state.[20]

Peticolas's remaining wartime service was less vigorous than his years in New Mexico and Louisiana. He appeared before the Army Medical Examination Board in Hempstead, Texas, during January 1864, and was declared "unfit for field service." A special order from headquarters, District of Texas, New Mexico, and Arizona, signed 1 February 1864, placed Peticolas on detached duty with the Quartermaster Department in Houston. There the young sergeant became a clerk in the office of the Chief Quartermaster for the remainder of his Civil War service. He apparently returned to his hometown after hostilities ended, for his name appears on the list of Confederate

18. Ibid., entry for 26 October 1863.

19. Ibid.

20. Noel, *A Campaign from Santa Fe to the Mississippi*, pp. xx, 143; Mark M. Boatner, III, *The Civil War Dictionary* (New York: David McKay, Co., 1959), pp. 685–89.

"Encampment of Provost Guard, 8th U. S., Co. A, in public square, Victoria, July 19th 1865." View looking south from the courthouse in the immediate postwar months. (Arizona Historical Society)

163

prisoners of war surrendered at Victoria prior to 8 August 1865.[21]

A. B. Peticolas's postwar career was as varied and successful as his wartime years had been exciting and adventurous. He resumed the practice of law in Victoria, as well as his friendships with several of the town's young women. Although he had no obvious favorites during the war, on 3 May 1866 he married Mary Dunbar, one of the young ladies who had so generously supplied him with clothing and best wishes when he was in Franklin, Texas, near the end of the New Mexico campaign. Alfred's time with Mary was brief, however; she and an infant daughter died less than two years later, on 11 October 1867, of yellow fever.[22]

Although he undoubtedly grieved for his deceased wife and baby, Peticolas's professional and social life went on. He continued his law partnership with Samuel A. White, and on 22 June 1869, Marion Goodwin became the second Mrs. Peticolas. Another of his Civil War benefactors, Marion was the daughter of Victoria's pioneer physician, Dr. Sherman H. Goodwin.[23]

Both Alfred and Marion Peticolas became leaders of Victoria civic and social activities. In addition, they were active in Presbyterian church affairs, and Mrs. Peticolas served at one time as president of the Federation of Women's Literary Clubs of Texas. They also had three sons. The first, Sherman Goodwin, was born on 1 July 1871, and was followed by Warner Marion in 1873 and Ralph Alfred in 1880.[24]

Peticolas's law practice grew rapidly during the post–Civil War years, and he eventually became one of the most respected and prominent attorneys in South Texas. During the 1880s, after much experience as a lawyer and judge, his courtroom technique was thus described:

> He was one of the old timers, and these were clever enough
> to capitalize even a physical infirmity. Mr. Peticolas was

21. Compiled Service Record, A. B. Peticolas, War Department Collection of Confederate Records, Cards No. 51909131, 50238913, 50239561, and 52800353, RG 109, NA; Elizabeth Bethel, comp., *Preliminary Inventory of the War Department Collection of Confederate Records* (Washington, D.C.: National Archives and Records Service, 1957), pp. 176–77.

22. Family Group Record, A. B. Peticolas and M. G. Peticolas. Copy in editor's collection.

23. Ibid.

24. Ibid.; Pedigree Chart and Peticolas Family Genealogy, Merrow E. Sorley, comp. Copy in editor's collection.

Judge A. B. Peticolas, ca. 1895. (Marian H. Martin Collection)

slightly deaf, and he so used same as to hear only evidence
that helped his case. By this process of infiltration the case
grew more Peticolas than precise, and drove opposing
counsel into a frenzy, and made perturbed witnesses
frantic. . . . The trial of a case was to him only a game, to
be fiercely played, sometimes by weird rules, but when the
cards fell, he collected his winnings, or paid his losses, with
a smile.[25]

In 1885, Peticolas combined his legal experience and penchant for
writing to produce his *Index Digest of Civil and Criminal Law of
Texas*, which was for many years a standard work in use by the Texas
bar. The author's preface to that book is in Aramaic, reflecting his
interest and reading in the history and literature of the Middle East
as well as, perhaps, a touch of Victorian pomposity.[26]

Love for the law remained with Peticolas throughout his life,
but many other interests and activities also vied for his attention.

25. *The Victoria Sesquicentennial "Scrapbook," 1824–1974* (Victoria, Texas: *Victoria Advocate*, 1974), p. 24.

26. Ibid.; Pedigree Chart and Peticolas Family Genealogy, Merrow E. Sorley, comp. Copy in editor's collection.

The Peticolas home in Victoria, Texas. (Marian H. Martin Collection)

He was an enthusiastic chess player from his days in the Confederate service. When not tied up in courtroom or office, "he played chess ubiquitously—at home, on trains, in his office—anybody, anywhere, and everywhere." He also found time to continue his sketching of scenes around Victoria and to become "a maker of exquisite cabinets." In addition, he had local banking and newspaper interests. For seven years (1881–87), he served as editor of the *Victoria Advocate*, writing literary criticism as well as editorials.[27]

The Peticolas home at the corner of Goodwin and Bridge streets was one of Victoria's showplaces. Its eloquent exterior was matched by the interior furnishings, which included, in the sitting room, a large portrait of Peticolas's mother. Here he and Marion entertained such groups as the Victoria Music Club and, on 7 November 1894, celebrated the first marriage of one of their sons by holding a reception for Warner M. Peticolas and his bride, Lola Davis.[28]

---

27. *Victoria Sesquicentennial "Scrapbook,"* p. 24; Shook, "A. B. Peticolas: 19th Century Victoria Artist," p. 11.

28. *Victoria Sesquicentennial "Scrapbook,"* p. 77; Family Group Record, A. B. Peticolas and M. G. Peticolas. Copy in editor's collection.

Of the three Peticolas sons, the oldest and youngest, Sherman G. and Ralph A., became prominent engineers and managers, while Warner M. Peticolas continued the family participation in the legal profession. After graduating from the University of Texas and practicing as an attorney in Victoria, he became the first chief justice of the Eighth Court of Appeals at El Paso, the youngest chief justice in the state.[29]

On 27 January 1915, the long, adventurous, and prosperous life of A. B. Peticolas, former sergeant of the Fourth Texas Mounted Volunteers, came to a peaceful end in Victoria. There, at Evergreen Cemetery, he and his wife Marion, who died five years later, were buried, leaving behind them a large and successful family and an enviable record of public service and professional excellence.[30]

---

29. Family Group Record, A. B. Peticolas and M. G. Peticolas; Pedigree Chart and Peticolas Family Genealogy, Merrow E. Sorley, comp.

30. Ibid.

Bibliography

Archival Collections

National Archives, Washington, D.C.
Records of the Secretary of State, Record Group 59
Territorial Papers, New Mexico
Records of the Adjutant General's Office, 1780s–1917, Record Group 94
Compiled Military Service Records
General Orders
Regimental Papers
Special Orders
Letters Received
Letters Sent
War Department Collection of Confederate Records, Record Group 109
Compiled Service Records
Records of the Hospital at Fort Fillmore and Doña Ana, New Mexico
Records of the Department of Texas and the Trans-Mississippi
Department
Records of Texas Troops
Records of Commands in Texas
Records of United States Army Continental Commands, 1821–1920,
Record Group 393
Letters Received
Letters Sent
Registers of Letters Received
Orders and General Orders
Special Orders
Field Records—New Mexico Volunteers
Records of the Quartermaster
Miscellaneous Records

Returns from U.S. Military Posts, 1800–1916, Microcopy 617
Letters Received by the Office of the Adjutant General, Main Series, 1861–70, Microcopy 619
Returns from Regular Army Cavalry Regiments, 1833–1916, Microcopy 744

State Records Center and Archives, Santa Fe, New Mexico
Adjutant General Files
    Annual Reports of the Adjutant General
    J. E. Farmer Diary
    Militia Description Book
    Miscellaneous Records and Muster Rolls
Territorial Papers

Texas State Library, Archives Division, Austin, Texas
Confederate Military Affairs, 1861–65

Government Publications

Bethel, Elizabeth. *Preliminary Inventory of the War Department Collection of Confederate Records, Record Group 109.* Washington, D.C.: National Archives and Records Service, 1957.

Everly, Elaine, et al., comp. *Preliminary Inventory of the Records of United States Army Continental Commands, 1821–1920, Record Group 393.* 5 vols. Washington, D.C.: National Archives and Record Service, 1973.

Munden, Kenneth W., and Henry P. Beers. *Guide to Federal Archives Relating to the Civil War.* Washington, D.C.: National Archives and Record Service, 1973.

Official Reports of Battles, Published by Order of the Confederate Congress at Richmond. New York: Charles B. Richardson, 1863.

The War of the Rebellion: A Compilation of the Official Records of the Union and Confederate Armies. Four Series, 128 vols. Washington, D.C.: Government Printing Office, 1880–1901.

Manuscript Materials

"Bugler," Co. B, Fifth New Mexico Volunteers. "Reminiscences of the Late War in New Mexico." Arrott Collection, New Mexico Highlands University, Las Vegas, N.M.

Chacon, Rafael. "Rafael Chacon Memoirs, 1832–1906." Translation in the collection of Jacqueline D. Meketa, Corrales, N.M.

Chivington, John M. "The First Colorado Regiment." Bancroft Library, University of California, Berkeley.

Collard, Felix R. "Reminiscences of a Private, Company 'G,' 7th Texas Cavalry, Sibley Brigade, CSA." Original journal in the collection of Dr. Robert F. Collard, Albuquerque, N.M.

Hanna, Ebenezer. "The Journal of Ebenezer Hanna." Texas State Library, Archives Division, Austin, Texas.

Howell, William R. "Journal of a Soldier of the Confederate States Army." Texas State Library, Archives Division, Austin. Typescript provided by Dr. Philip L. Mead, Albuquerque, N.M.

McCleave, William A. "Recollections of a California Volunteer." Bancroft Library, University of California, Berkeley.

Merrick, M. Wolfe. "Notes and Sketches of Campaigns in New Mexico, Arizona, Texas, Louisana, and Arkansas by a Participant, Dr. M. W. Merrick, from Feb. 16, 1861, to May 26, 1865; Actual Service in the Field." Texas History Research Library of the Daughters of the Republic of Texas, The Alamo, San Antonio.

Miller, John D. Letter to Father, 3 April 1862. Arrott Collection, New Mexico Highlands University, Las Vegas, N.M. Miller was a trooper in Co. F, First Colorado Volunteers.

Peticolas, Alfred B. "Journal of A. B. Peticolas, May–July 1859." Local History Collection, Victoria College, Victoria, Texas.

———. "Journal of A. B. Peticolas, 21 February–15 June 1862." Volumes 2 and 3 in collection of William C. Peticolas, El Paso, Texas.

———. License to Practice Law, Amherst County Court, Virginia, 24 August 1859. Local History Collection, Victoria College, Victoria, Texas.

Peticolas, Alfred B., and Marion G. Family Group Record. In the collection of Marian H. Martin, Azle, Texas.

Sorley, Merrow E., comp. Pedigree Chart and Peticolas Family Genealogy. In the collection of Marian H. Martin, Azle, Texas.

Trujillo, Julian J. Letter to C. A. Deane, Denver, Colo., 9 May 1898, Subject: Recovery of Buried Cannons. Archives, Colorado Historical Association, Denver.

Wright, H. C. "Reminiscences of H. C. Wright of Austin." Library, University of Texas, Austin.

Dissertations and Theses

Felgar, Robert P. "Texas in the War for Southern Independence, 1861–1865." Ph.D. dissertation, University of Texas, 1935.

Hall, Martin H. "Confederate Military Operations in Arizona and New Mexico." M.A. thesis, University of Alabama, 1951.

———. "The Army of New Mexico: Sibley's Campaign of 1862." Ph.D. dissertation, Louisiana State University, 1957.

Killin, Hugh E. "The Texans and the California Column." M.A. thesis, Texas Technological College, 1931.

Kroh, Robert F. "Tom Green: Shield and Buckler." M.A. thesis, University of Texas, 1951.

Miller, Darlis A. "General James Henry Carleton in New Mexico, 1862–1867." M.A. thesis, New Mexico State University, 1970.

———. "A Civil War Legacy: Californians in New Mexico." Ph.D. dissertation, University of New Mexico, 1977.

Rogan, Francis E. "Military History of New Mexico During the Civil War." Ph.D. dissertation, University of Utah, 1961.

Taylor, Albion, Jr. "Military Operations in Texas During the Civil War." M.A. thesis, Baylor University, 1931.

Waldrop, William I. "New Mexico During the Civil War." M.A. thesis, University of New Mexico, 1950.

Whitworth, Bonnye R. "The Role of Texas in the Confederacy." M.A. thesis, North Texas State College, 1951.

Newspapers

Chronicle (Houston)
Countryman (Bellville, Texas)
Daily Herald (El Paso)
The Fort Brown Flag (Brownsville, Texas)
Gazette (Las Vegas, New Mexico)
Herald (San Antonio, Texas)
Mesilla Times (New Mexico)
The National Tribune (Washington, D.C.)
New Mexico Press (Albuquerque)
Rocky Mountain News (Denver)
Santa Fe Daily New Mexican
Santa Fe New Mexican
Santa Fe Weekly Gazette
State Gazette (Austin)
Rio Abajo Weekly Press (Albuquerque)
Tri-Weekly Telegraph (Houston)
Victoria Advocate (Texas)

Books and Pamphlets

Agnew, Stanley C. *Garrisons of the Regular U.S. Army: New Mexico 1846–1899*. Santa Fe: Press of the Territorian, 1971.

———. *Garrisons of the Regular U.S. Army: Arizona 1851–1899*. Arlington, Va.: Council on Abandoned Military Posts, 1974.

Ashcraft, Allan C. *Texas in the Civil War: A Resumé History*. Austin: Texas Civil War Centennial Commission, 1962.

Barr, Alwynn. *Charles Porter's Account of the Confederate Attempt to Seize Arizona and New Mexico*. Austin: Pemberton Press, 1964.

172

Boatner, Mark M., III. *The Civil War Dictionary*. New York: David McKay Co., 1959.

Chavez, Tibo J., and Gilberto Espinosa. *El Rio Abajo*. Portales, N.M.: Bishop Publishing Co., n.d.

Colton, Ray C. *The Civil War in the Western Territories*. Norman: University of Oklahoma Press, 1959.

Craig, Reginald S. *The Fighting Parson: The Biography of Colonel John M. Chivington*. Los Angeles: Westernlore Press, 1959.

Cullum, George W. *Biographical Register of the Officers and Graduates of the United States Military Academy*. 3 vols. Boston: Houghton, Mifflin and Co., 1891. Supplement, 1890–1900 as Vol. 4.

Dornbusch, C. E. *Military Bibliography of the Civil War*. 3 vols. New York: Arms Press, 1971.

Edwards, William B. *Civil War Guns*. Harrisburg, Penn.: Stackpole Company, 1962.

Emmett, Chris. *Fort Union and the Winning of the Southwest*. Norman: University of Oklahoma Press, 1965.

Farber, James. *Texas, C.S.A.* New York: Jackson Co., 1947.

Faulk, Odie B. *General Tom Green, Fightin' Texan*. Waco: Texian Press, 1963.

Ferriss, Robert G., ed. *Soldier and Brave*. National Survey of Historic Sites and Buildings, Vol. 12. Washington, D.C.: National Park Service, 1971.

Fisher, Margaret M. *Utah and the Civil War*. Salt Lake City: Deseret Book Co., 1929.

Fitzpatrick, Francis E. *History of Fort Wingate Depot, Forts Fauntleroy and Lyon*. Gallup, N.M.: published by author, n.d.

Frazer, Robert W. *Forts of the West*. Norman: University of Oklahoma Press, 1965.

Fuller, Claud E., and Roland D. Steuart. *Firearms of the Confederacy*. Lawrence, Mass.: Quarterman Publications, 1944.

Ganaway, Loomis M. *New Mexico and the Sectional Controversy, 1846–1861*. Albuquerque: University of New Mexico Press, 1944.

Giese, Dale F., ed. *My Life with the Army in the West, The Memoirs of James E. Farmer, 1858–1898*. Santa Fe: Stagecoach Press, 1967.

Grinstead, Marion C. *Life and Death of a Frontier Fort: Fort Craig, New Mexico, 1854–1885*. Socorro, N.M.: Socorro County Historical Society, 1973.

Hall, Martin H. *The Confederate Army of New Mexico*. Austin: Presidial Press, 1978.

———. *Sibley's New Mexico Campaign*. Austin: University of Texas Press,, 1960.

Hart, Herbert M. *Old Forts of the Far West*. New York: Bonanza Books, 1965.

———. *Old Forts of the Southwest*. Seattle: Superior Publishing Co., 1964.

———. *Tour Guide to Old Western Forts*. Ft. Collins, Colo.: Old Army Press, 1980.

Henderson, Harry M. *Texas in the Confederacy.* San Antonio: Naylor Co., 1955.

Heyman, Max L., Jr. *Prudent Soldier: A Biography of Major General E. R. S. Canby, 1817–1873.* . . . Glendale, Calif.: Arthur H. Clark Co., 1959.

Hollister, Ovando J. *Boldly They Rode.* 1863. Reprint. Lakewood, Colo.: Golden Press, 1949.

Horn, Calvin. *New Mexico's Troubled Years.* Albuquerque: Horn and Wallace Publishers, 1963.

Horn, Calvin, and William S. Wallace, eds. *Confederate Victories in the Southwest: Prelude to Defeat.* Albuquerque: Horn and Wallace Publishers, 1961.

———. *Union Army Operations in the Southwest: Final Victory.* Albuquerque: Horn and Wallace Publishers, 1961.

Hunt, Aurora. *The Army of the Pacific.* Glendale, Calif.: Arthur H. Clark Co., 1951.

———. *Major General James Henry Carleton, 1814–1873: Western Frontier Dragoon.* Glendale, Calif.: Arthur H. Clark Co., 1958.

Ickis, Alonzo F. *Bloody Trails Along the Rio Grande: A Day-by-Day Diary of Alonzo Ferdinand Ickis.* Edited by Nolie Mumey. Denver: Fred A. Rosenstock, 1958.

Johnson, Byron A., ed. *Early Albuquerque.* Albuquerque: Journal Publishing Co., 1981.

———. *Old Town, Albuquerque, New Mexico, A Guide to Its History and Architecture.* Albuquerque: Albuquerque Museum, 1980.

Johnson, Sid S. *Texans Who Wore the Gray.* Tyler, Texas: n.p., 1907.

Keleher, William A. *Turmoil in New Mexico.* Santa Fe: Rydal Press, 1952.

Kerby, Robert L. *The Confederate Invasion of New Mexico and Arizona, 1861–1862.* Los Angeles: Westernlore Press, 1958.

Ladd, Horatio. *The Story of New Mexico.* Boston: D. Lathy Co., 1891.

Long, E. B. *The Civil War Day by Day: An Almanac 1861–1865.* Garden City: Doubleday and Co., 1971.

Marchand, Ernest, ed. *News from Fort Craig, New Mexico, 1863, Civil War Letters of Andrew Ryan, with the First California Volunteers.* Santa Fe: Stagecoach Press, 1966.

McKee, James C. *Narrative of the Surrender of a Command of U.S. Forces, at Fort Fillmore, New Mexico in July, A.D., 1861.* Boston: John A. Lowell, 1886.

Meketa, Charles and Jacqueline D. *One Blanket and Ten Days Rations.* Globe, Ariz.: Southwest Parks and Monuments Association, 1980.

Meketa, Jacqueline D. *Louis Felsenthal: Citizen Soldier of Territorial New Mexico.* Albuquerque: University of New Mexico Press, 1982.

Miller, Darlis A. *The California Column in New Mexico.* Albuquerque: University of New Mexico Press, 1982.

Nankivell, John H. *History of the Military Organizations of the State of Colorado, 1860–1935.* Denver: Kestler Stationery Co., 1935.

Noel, Theophilus. *A Campaign from Santa Fe to the Mississippi: Being a History of the Old Sibley Brigade.* . . . Edited by Martin H. Hall and Edwin A. Davis. 1865. Reprint. Houston: Stagecoach Press, 1961.

Pearce, T. M., ed. *New Mexico Place Names.* Albuquerque: University of New Mexico Press, 1965.

Pettis, George H. *The California Column: Its Campaigns and Service in New Mexico, Arizona and Texas.* Santa Fe: New Mexico Historical Society, 1908.

————. *Personal Narratives of Events in the War of the Rebellion.* . . . Providence, R.I.: Soldier's and Sailor's Historical Society of Rhode Island, 1885.

Prince, L. Bradford. *Old Fort Marcy, Santa Fe, New Mexico.* Santa Fe: New Mexican Printing Co., 1912.

Rittenhouse, Jack D. *New Mexico Civil War Bibliography.* Houston: Stagecoach Press, 1960.

Rodenbough, Theophilus F. *From Everglade to Cañon With the Second Dragoons.* New York: D. Van Nostrand, 1875. Lt. Joseph M. Bell contributed an account of the Battle of Valverde.

Rodenbough, Theophilus F., and William L. Haskin, eds. *The Army of the United States.* 1896. Reprint. New York: Argonaut Press, 1966.

Rose, Victor M. *Some Historical Facts in Regard to the Settlement of Victoria, Texas: Its Progress and Present Status.* 1883. Reprint. Victoria: Book Mart, 1961.

Scobee, Barry. *Old Fort Davis.* San Antonio: Naylor Co., 1947.

Simmons, Marc. *Albuquerque: A Narrative History.* Albuquerque: University of New Mexico Press, 1982.

————. *New Mexico: A Bicentennial History.* New York: Norton, 1977.

————. *The Little Lion of the Southwest: A Life of Manuel Antonio Chavez.* Chicago: Sage Books, 1973.

Stanley, F. [Crocchiola, Stanley F. L.] *The Civil War in New Mexico.* Denver: World Press, 1960.

————. *The Glorieta, New Mexico, Story.* Pep, Texas: n.p., 1965.

————. *Fort Craig.* Pampa, Texas: n.p., 1963.

————. *Fort Stanton.* Pampa, Texas: Pampa Print Shop, 1964.

————. *Fort Union.* Denver: World Press, 1953.

Straw, Mary J. *Loretto: The Sisters and Their Santa Fe Chapel.* Santa Fe: Loretto Chapel, 1983.

Taylor, Richard. *Destruction and Reconstruction: Personal Experiences of the Late War.* Edited by Richard B. Howell. 1879. Reprint. New York: Longmans, Green and Co., 1955.

Twitchell, Ralph E. *The Leading Facts of New Mexican History.* 5 vols. Cedar Rapids: Torch Press, 1911–17.

Utley, Robert M. *Fort Davis National Historic Site, Texas.* National Park

Service Historical Handbook Series. Washington, D.C.: Government Printing Office, 1965.

———. *Fort Union National Monument, New Mexico.* National Park Service Historical Handbook Series. Washington, D.C.: Government Printing Office, 1962.

———. *Frontiersmen in Blue: The United States Army and the Indian, 1840–1865.* New York: Macmillan Co., 1967.

The Victoria Sesquicentennial "Scrapbook," 1824–1974. Victoria, Texas: *Victoria Advocate*, 1974.

Webb, Walter P., and H. Bailey Carroll, eds. *The Handbook of Texas.* 2 vols. Austin: Texas State Historical Association, 1952.

Whitford, William C. *Colorado Volunteers in the Civil War, The New Mexico Campaign in 1862.* 1906. Reprint. Boulder, Colo.: Pruett Press, 1963; and Glorieta, N.M.: Rio Grande Press, 1971.

Williams, Ellen. *Three Years and a Half in the Army; or History of the Second Colorados.* New York: Fowler and Wells Co., 1885.

Winsor, Bill. *Texas in the Confederacy: Military Installations, Economy and People.* Hillsboro, Texas: Hill Junior College Press, 1978.

Wright, Arthur A. *The Civil War in the Southwest.* Denver: Big Mountain Press, 1964.

Articles

Alberts, Don E. "The Battle of Peralta." *New Mexico Historical Review* 58 (October 1983): 369–79.

Anderson, Hattie M. "With the Confederates in New Mexico During the Civil War: Memoirs of Hank Smith." *Panhandle Plains Historical Review* 2 (1929): 65–97.

Anderson, Latham. "Canby's Services in the New Mexico Campaign." In *Battles and Leaders of the Civil War.* 4 vols. 1884–88. Reprint. New York: Yoseloff, 1956. Vol. 2: 697–99.

Barbaras, Richard, and Casandra Richard. "Sibley's Retreat." *Rio Grande History* 11 (1980): 2–3.

Barr, Alwynn. "A Bibliography of Articles on the Military History of Texas." *Texas Military History* 3 (1963): 265–74, and subsequent issues to 6 (Spring 1967).

Bell, Joseph M. "The Campaign of New Mexico." In *War Papers Read Before the Commandery of the State of Wisconsin, Military Order of the Loyal Legion of the United States.* 8 vols. Milwaukee: Burdick, Armitage and Allen, 1891. Vol. 1: 47–71.

Bender, A. B. "Frontier Defense in the Territory of New Mexico, 1853–1861." *New Mexico Historical Review* 9 (October 1934): 345–73.

Bloom, Lansing B., ed. "Confederate Reminiscences of 1862." *New Mexico Historical Review* 5 (July 1930): 315–24.

Bryan, Howard. "The Man Who Buried the Cannons." *New Mexico Magazine* 40 (January 1962): 13–15, 35.

Burton, Estelle B. "Volunteer Soldiers of New Mexico and Their Conflicts with the Indians in 1862 and 1863." *Old Santa Fe* 1 (1914): 386–419.

Clendenin, Clarence C. "General James Henry Carleton." *New Mexico Historical Review* 30 (January 1955): 23–43.

Crimmins, M. L., contrib. "The Battle of Val Verde." *New Mexico Historical Review* 7 (October 1932): 348–52.

———. "Fort Fillmore." *New Mexico Historical Review* 6 (October 1931): 327–33.

Darrow, Caroline B. "Recollections of the Twiggs Surrender." In *Battles and Leaders of the Civil War.* 4 vols. 1884–88. Reprint. New York: Yoseloff, 1956. Vol. 1: 33–39.

Donnell, F. S. "The Confederate Territory of Arizona, from Official Sources." *New Mexico Historical Review* 17 (April 1942): 148–63.

———. "When Las Vegas Was the Capital of New Mexico." *New Mexico Historical Review* 8 (July 1933): 265–72.

———. "When Texas Owned New Mexico to the Rio Grande." *New Mexico Historical Review* 8 (April 1933): 65–75.

Eaton, W. Clemment. "Frontier Life in Southern Arizona, 1858–1861." *Southwestern Historical Quarterly* 36 (January 1933): 173–92.

Evans, A. W. "Canby at Valverde." In *Battles and Leaders of the Civil War.* 4 vols. 1884–88. Reprint. New York: Yoseloff, 1956. Vol. 2: 699–700.

Faulkner, Walter A., contrib. "With Sibley in New Mexico; The Journal of William Henry Smith." *West Texas Historical Association Year Book* 27 (October 1951): 111–42.

Gilbert, Benjamin F. "The Confederate Minority in California." *California Historical Society Quarterly* 20 (June 1941): 154–70.

Gracey, David B., II, ed. "New Mexico Campaign Letters of Frank Starr, 1861–1862." *Texas Military History* 4 (Fall 1964): 169–88.

Gregg, Andrew K. "The Battle of Albuquerque." *Impact* 5 February 1980: 10–12.

Haas, Oscar, trans. "The Diary of Julius Giesecke." *Texas Military History* 3 (Winter 1963): 228–42.

Hall, Martin H. "An Appraisal of the 1862 New Mexico Campaign: A Confederate Officer's Letter to Nacogdoches." *New Mexico Historical Review* 51 (October 1976): 329–33.

———. "The First Colorado Regiment." *New Mexico Historical Review* 33 (April 1958): 144–54.

———. "Captain John G. Phillips' 'Brigands.'" *Military History of Texas and the Southwest* 11 (1973): 131–35.

———. "Native Mexican Relations in Confederate Arizona, 1861–1862." *Journal of Arizona History* 8 (Autumn 1967): 171–78.

Hayes, A. A. "The New Mexico Campaign of 1862." *Magazine of American History* 15 (February 1886): 171–84.

Holden, W. C. "Frontier Defense in Texas During the Civil War." *West Texas Historical Association Year Book* 4 (June 1928): 16–31.

Howard, James A., II. "New Mexico and Arizona Territories." *Journal of the West* 16 (April 1977): 85–100.

Hunsaker, William J. "Lansford W. Hastings' Project for the Invasion and Conquest of Arizona and New Mexico for the Southern Confederacy." *Arizona Historical Review* 4 (July 1931): 5–12.

McCoy, Raymond. "The Battle of Glorieta Pass." *United Daughters of the Confederacy Magazine* 15 (February 1952): 12–13, 23.

———. "Confederate Cannon." *New Mexico Magazine* 31 (September 1953): 18, 49.

McMaster, Richard K., and George Ruhlen. "The Guns of Valverde." *Password* 5 (1960): 20–34.

Miller, Darlis A. "Carleton's California Column: A Chapter in New Mexico's Mining History." *New Mexico Historical Review* 53 (January 1978): 5–38.

———. "Hispanos and the Civil War in New Mexico: A Reconsideration." *New Mexico Historical Review* 54 (April 1979): 105–23.

———. "Historian for the California Column: George H. Petis of New Mexico and Rhode Island." *Red River Valley Historical Review* 5 (Winter 1980): 74–92.

Mumey, Nolie. "John Minton Chivington, The Misunderstood Man." *Brand Book of the Denver Westerners* (1956): 54–60.

Myers, Lee. "New Mexico Volunteers, 1862–1866." *The Smoke Signal* 37 (Spring 1979): 138–52.

Pettis, George H. "The Confederate Invasion of New Mexico and Arizona." In *Battles and Leaders of the Civil War*. 4 vols. 1884–88. Reprint. New York: Yoseloff, 1956. Vol. 2: 103–11.

Quenzel, Carrol H. "General Henry Hopkins Sibley: Military Inventor." *Virginia Magazine of History and Biography* 64 (April 1956): 166–76.

Rippy, J. Fred. "Mexican Projects of the Confederates." *Southwestern Historical Quarterly* 22 (April 1919): 291–317.

Rodgers, Robert L. "The Confederate States Organized Arizona in 1862." *Southern Historical Society Papers* 28 (1900): 222–27.

Santee, J. F. "The Battle of La Glorieta Pass." *New Mexico Historical Review* 6 (January 1931): 66–75.

Schreier, Konrad F., Jr. "The California Column in the Civil War, Hazen's Civil War Diary." *Journal of San Diego History* 22 (Spring 1976): 31–48.

Shook, Robert W. "A. B. Peticolas: 19th Century Victoria Artist." *Victoria College Kaleidoscope* (Spring 1979): 10–12.

Smith, C. C. "Some Unpublished History of the Southwest." *Arizona Historical Review* 4 (July 1931): 13–38.

Teel, Trevanion T. "Sibley's New Mexican Campaign: Its Object and the Causes of Its Failure." In *Battles and Leaders of the Civil War*. 4 vols. 1884–88. Reprint. New York: Yoseloff, 1956. Vol. 2: 700.

Thompson, Jerry D. "Mexican-Americans in the Civil War: The Battle of Valverde." *Texana* 10 (1972): 23–35.

Tittman, Edward D. "Confederate Courts in New Mexico." *New Mexico Historical Review* 3 (October 1928): 128–45.

Utley, Robert M. "Fort Union and the Santa Fe Trail." *New Mexico Historical Review* 36 (January 1961): 36–48.

Waldrip, William I. "New Mexico During the Civil War." *New Mexico Historical Review* 28 (October 1953): 163–82, 251–90.

Walker, Charles S., Jr. "Causes of the Confederate Invasion of New Mexico." *New Mexico Historical Review* 8 (April 1933): 76–97.

———. "Confederate Government in Doña Ana County as Shown in the Records of the Probate Court, 1861–1862." *New Mexico Historical Review* 6 (July 1931): 252–302.

Walker, Henry P., ed. "Soldier in the California Column: The Diary of John W. Teal." *Arizona and the West* 13 (Spring 1971): 33–82.

Wallace, R. B. "My Experiences in the First Colorado Regiment." *Colorado Magazine* 1 (November 1924): 307–12.

Waller, J. L. "The Civil War in the El Paso Area." *West Texas Historical Association Year Book* 22 (October 1946): 3–14.

Watford, W. H. "Confederate Western Ambitions." *Southwestern Historical Quarterly* 44 (October 1940): 161–87.

———. "The Far-Western Wing of the Rebellion." *California Historical Society Quarterly* 34 (June 1955): 125–48.

Index